TOUGH QUESTIONS – GOOD ANSWERS

**Other Titles in the Capital
Business & Personal Development Series:**

TOUGH QUESTIONS – GOOD ANSWERS

Taking Control of Any Interview

THOMAS F. CALCAGNI

Capital Ideas for Business & Personal Development

CAPITAL
BOOKS, INC.
Sterling, Virginia

Capital Books, Inc.
P.O. Box 605
Herndon, Virginia 20172-0605

ISBN 13: 978-1-933102-50-4

Library of Congress Cataloging-in-Publication Data

Calcagni, Thomas F.
  Tough questions—good answers : taking control of any interview / Thomas F. Calcagni.
  p. cm. — (Capital ideas for business & personal development series)
  ISBN 978-1-933102-50-4 (alk. paper)
  1. Interpersonal communication. 2. Interviews. 3. Public speaking. I. Title. II. Series.

  HM1166.C35 2007
  808.5'1—dc22

                                        2007022875

Illustrations by Elizabeth Calcagni

Printed in the United States of America on acid-free paper that meets the American National Standards Institute Z39-48 Standard.

First Edition

10 9 8 7 6 5 4 3 2 1

To my parents, Marian and Frank Calcagni,
for their encouragement and unconditional love,
and to my wife, Liz,
for her understanding, partnership, love, and invaluable
contributions to making this book possible.

CONTENTS

FOREWORD

Information is the lifeblood of any enterprise. Without it, corporations, associations, and governments cannot make the best decisions for their customers, members, or constituents. But gathering information is only half the battle. Whether it is a product, service, or idea, most organizations have a need to communicate what they do and to encourage the public to take action as a result, whether it is buying a new car or supporting a piece of Congressional legislation.

Many of these organizations rely on advertising to deliver their messages directly to consumers or stakeholders, while others prefer, or can only afford, to communicate with their target audiences through news coverage and the Internet. With so many messages competing for the attention of readers, listeners, and viewers, however, it can be extraordinarily difficult and frustrating to break through all of this "noise." That is why many organizations turn to public relations consultants to help them craft exactly the right communications messages. They hope these messages will generate significant media coverage for their company, product, or issue with the goal of influencing the behavior of the audiences they want to reach.

So what does this tell us? Sophisticated companies and organizations understand the importance of developing clear, concise communication messages. And, they use them to explain who they are and why people should buy their products or support their causes. Fortunately, good communications messaging is a skill that does not only belong to the rich and powerful. It is a skill that can be used by everyday people on the job or in their daily lives to become more persuasive and effective communicators. *Tough Questions—Good Answers* not only shows readers how to create their own personal communications messages, but also gives practical advice on how to use messages to answer hard questions in almost any personal or professional situation.

As the former director of the federal government's Office of Personnel Management, in the Clinton administration, I faced tough questions from congressional representatives, administration officials, the media, staff, and federal workers nearly every day. I can tell you from personal experience, knowing your messages before going into any kind of meeting where you are going to be asked questions will improve greatly your chances of success.

Tom Calcagni shows you what every successful executive and politician knows when faced with tough questions. He shows you how to use your messages to reinforce the points you want to make and how to use your messages to deflect questions you do not want to answer. With *Tough Questions—Good Answers,* you will learn how to develop your own personal communications messages and how to use them successfully in every facet of your life.

Janice R. Lachance
Chief Executive Officer
Special Libraries Association

ACKNOWLEDGMENTS

I thank *Capital Books*, especially publisher Kathleen Hughes and my editor, Amy Fries, who supported my vision in this endeavor. Their commitment, combined with their creative talent and support, was unwavering and greatly appreciated.

I thank a friend and former colleague, Sandy Trupp, vice president of Planned Television Arts, a division of Ruder Finn Washington, for the time she spent reviewing early drafts of my manuscript. As an accomplished communications consultant and author, her feedback and suggestions were invaluable.

I thank my family, especially Liz, for being my wife, friend, and business partner. I also thank our children Deane, Gretchen, Ted, Jerry, Chris, Gina, and Lisa for their support and encouragement.

And finally, I thank my friends who gave me feedback on the manuscript, Wendy Justice and Georgie Goldston, and my colleagues and friends who made contributions to this book in their own individual ways: Janice Lachance, Nancy Sansalone, Doug Newcomb, Linda Broussard, Cara Battaglini, Stephen Davis, Kim Rutherford, Shelley Angers, Melanie Miller, Amy Binder, Don Rheem, Kristine Heine, Helen Sramak, Jim Harff, Bruce Harrison, Adam Sohn, Celia Rocks, Mark Franz, Angela de

Rocha, David Trevett, Jim Condon, Jon DeWitt, Bill Melton, John Miller, Kathy Barnsdorf, Toby Knox, Susan Pikrallidas, Geoff Sundstrom, Mantill Williams, Janie Graziani, Aymee Ruiz, Justin McNaull, Sue Farley, and the late Jerry Cheske.

INTRODUCTION

What would you give to go into any job interview, sales call, employee review, or presentation with confidence, knowing that whatever question is thrown at you, you'll be able to handle it? You'd give a lot—if you're like most of us.

There's no need to fear tough questions; you just have to learn how to handle them. But to do that, you must know how to create strong communications messages and understand how to deliver them effectively if you want to make yourself more successful. That's what *Tough Questions—Good Answers* will teach you to do.

If you're already thinking this is too good to be true, I applaud your skepticism. When I was a graduate student at Northwestern University's Medill School of Journalism, we had a saying, "If your mother says she loves you, check it out." But I'm confident if you "check out" the techniques in *Tough Questions—Good Answers*, you won't find them too good to be true; you'll find them easy to use and highly effective in your everyday communication with friends, family, and business associates.

As a communications consultant, I've had the good fortune to work with many senior executives at public and private companies and at nationally recognized associations, a couple of United States senators, and even a legendary NASCAR driver. And I've learned an interesting thing. Most organization presidents and chief executive officers, people with enormous power over the lives of hundreds or thousands of employees, men and women of great talent and accomplishment, don't look forward to answering questions from reporters any more than you enjoy answering questions from your boss, a loan officer, or an angry employee.

In fact, it may be even worse for these highly accomplished executives because they're used to being in control of nearly any situation. That's not the case when faced with tough questions from pesky, independent-minded reporters. So these hardened business pros often turn to people like me to help them prepare for interviews and, more importantly, to learn how to take control of them.

"Wait just a minute," I can hear you say, "What do you mean 'take control of an interview?' You just said these exectutives aren't in control when faced with a tough interview." That's right; they're not. But they can learn to control the *direction* of an interview and, ultimately, its outcome by employing the techniques in this book. More importantly, you can learn to do the same thing even if you're not talking with a member of the Fourth Estate.

It may surprise you to learn that I use these techniques all the time in business and in my personal life. With the help of the simple techniques described in *Tough Questions—Good Answers* and a little practice, you'll develop the confidence and skill you need to answer any type of question effectively, no matter how difficult, and ensure that the important ideas YOU want to express are heard.

Tom Calcagni
tcalcagni@toughquestionsgoodanswers.com

CHAPTER ONE

THE CONFIDENCE FACTOR

Confidence is a funny thing. With it, you can do just about anything. But without it, you might as well "forgetaboutit," as they say in New Jersey. That's because accomplishment usually flows from the belief that you can do something well. That's especially true when it comes to performing. Whether you're performing on a Broadway stage, on an athletic field, or in front of a group of business executives, confidence can make the difference between a brilliant performance or a forgettable one. Let's face it, some people are born with more than their fair share of confidence. But most people aren't. What gives most of us the confidence we need to do something well is preparation and practice.

A former business partner of mine was a very good golfer. He was captain of the golf team at the prep school he attended and eventually earned a golf scholarship to a prestigious university. One day we were talking about what it takes to be successful at the game of golf. While he could have given me an in-depth explanation about the mechanics of a good swing or talked at length about the importance of concentration and focus, he didn't. Instead, he told me his dad used to take him out to the local golf course and immediately throw his ball into the rough. His father did this over and over again. "Why?" I asked. "Simple," my friend said. "My dad knew that if I had the confidence to hit the ball no matter where it landed, imagine how fearlessly I could hit it from the tee." Makes perfect sense to me.

While most of us recognize the importance of preparation and practice, we don't apply it to all things. How many of us as kids practiced a musical instrument for hours or took part in football, baseball, or soccer practice after school? That seemed like such a natural thing at the time, and our performance improved because of it. But interestingly, most of us never give much thought to the idea of preparing and practicing to answer questions. Maybe it's because we answer them all the time, and it seems as effortless as breathing: "What's your name?" "Where are you from?" "How would you like your eggs?" Easy questions, easy answers.

But what happens when the questions get tougher . . . when the answers make a real difference? Suppose your answers will determine whether you land or keep a job? What if they will make the difference between your company's success or failure? In these situations, your answers matter, and your ability to answer well will depend largely on preparation and practice.

Like it or not, answering questions is a performance art. And, as we all learned on our first day of kindergarten, "Practice makes perfect."

Practice, by the way, doesn't have to be drudgery. Some of my happiest memories as a kid are of scooping up ground balls hour after hour thrown to me by my very patient father in the street in front of our suburban Chicago home. That was practice, and it was fun. While preparing and practicing to answer questions may not be as fun as practicing a sport, it can be just as invigorating. It poses a mental challenge that, once met, will pay dividends for years to come.

CHAPTER TWO

MESSAGES:
THE GUIDING LIGHT

CHAPTER MESSAGES

What: Messages are the key points you want to communicate based upon an identifiable goal.

How: By clearly and concisely delivering your messages, you focus on the key thoughts you wish to impress upon your listener.

Why: Three well-thought-out messages allow you to take control of any meeting, interview, or conversation. Whether you're a parent communicating with teenagers or a CEO directing a large organization, messages allow you to communicate consistently what you think is important.

When you learn to play the piano, you begin by practicing scales. When you learn to answer questions effectively, you begin by developing communications messages. "Communications messages," that's a fancy way of saying, "What are the points I want to make?" If you don't know what you want to say, you certainly can't say it well. But you would be surprised to learn how many people go into a board meeting, job interview, or employee evaluation without thinking through what they want to communicate.

"What does that have to do with answering questions?" you may ask. Everything! You see, questions provide us with the opportunity not only to answer, but also to take control of the conversation.

Think of it this way. There are two parts to every answer. The information or opinion you've been asked to give and the message you want to deliver. You probably answer questions this way all the time without really thinking about it. If I ask you, "Are you hungry?" you may say, "Yes." I've asked you a simple question, and you've given me a simple answer. But you may not stop there. If you want to go out to dinner, you may add, "Hey, let's go get some ribs."

What you've done is you've answered the question AND delivered a message that's important to you. Yes, you're hungry, but, more importantly, you want ribs. In effect, you've taken control of the conversation by your answer to a rather innocuous question.

While this is a very simplistic example, you can apply this same approach to any personal or business conversation or interview. By answering a question, then continuing to use your answer to communicate what you really want to say, you can subtly direct the conversation in the direction in which you want it to go.

Massaging Your Messages

Using communications messages effectively requires preplanning. First and foremost, you need to know what it is you want to communicate. And THAT depends on what you hope to accomplish.

Not too long ago, someone I know was looking for a public relations job. He had good credentials, but also had changed jobs a lot. While "job hopping" is commonplace among today's public relations professionals, he knew his job history would likely raise red flags for prospective employers. He wrote down the three most important things he wanted employers to know about him, keeping in mind he'd have to address the numerous jobs he'd held. His first message focused on his experience in many different areas of public relations and how that experience would make him a good fit for the job. Message two offered the reasons he'd like to find a job he could stay in for many years. But message three was probably the most important. It addressed the issue of job hopping by emphasizing that he wouldn't have had the expertise he had to offer the company if he hadn't changed jobs frequently thus enhancing his skills and experience. It worked. He landed the job and lived happily ever after, at least so far.

Messages work in almost any situation, if you take the time to figure out what you want someone else to know.

Okay, if you haven't guessed it by now, I was the candidate. My point in telling this story is: Messages work in almost any situation, if you take the time to figure out what you want someone else to know.

Once you figure that out, it doesn't take long to craft the messages that will have the effect you desire.

How many communications messages should you have in any given situation? That's up to you. But as a rule of thumb, I suggest no more than three. Why three? While I could probably consult mystics and conduct extensive research in the bowels of the Vatican searching for spiritual and psychological explanations for the significance of the number three, the simple answer is this: Three messages seem to work. Having coached many executives of public and private companies, I realized over time that they could easily remember and work with three messages, and three messages were usually enough to make the points they wanted to make. We'll talk about what should be included in these messages in the next section.

Messages are not intended to contain every piece of information or every last bit of data you have in your head. They're intended to focus your thinking on the important ideas you wish to convey. If it's important for me to know we're having a thunderstorm, you can tell me that without explaining that thunderstorms are caused by the uplifting of warm, moist, unstable air. While that may be quite interesting, what I really need to understand is that I'll probably get drenched and possibly struck by lightning if I go outside during the storm.

I don't want to leave you with the impression, however, that detail isn't important. Unquestionably, it is. But good communication lies in the ability to convey essential information quickly, in a way that's easy to understand. Once you've done that, you can provide all the necessary detail you want during follow-up questions.

Earlier, I pointed out that one of my messages during a job hunt focused on my broad communications expertise, thanks to the numerous jobs I have held. Unless I was prepared to bore my interviewers to death, I couldn't talk about each and every job as part of my message. Nevertheless, in response to follow-up questions, I was able to provide specifics about my job history and to offer the necessary substantiation the interviewers sought.

So even though you only have three messages, you'll likely need a fist full of facts to make your case. But let the facts be the supporting actors in your play. The starring roles belong to your messages.

The Who, What, Where, When, and Why of Identifying Messages

If you're with me so far, I hope you're asking yourself, "How do I invest in this message thing—it's going to be hotter than high tech?" Okay, that may be a little exaggerated, but it can make you a better communicator.

Up to this point, I've talked about the need for messages and why they're important. Now it's time to take a closer look at creating them. For some people, coming up with messages is almost second nature. I'm not one of those people. I have to think about what I want to say, and I often have to write it down. So if you're like me, where do you begin?

Obviously, what you say depends on what you want to accomplish. Whether it's going out for ribs or convincing a prospective employer to hire you, your goals will determine your messages. Every goal is different, of course, but I would like to explain an approach to crafting messages that has worked successfully for me time and again over the years. Interestingly, it's the same technique employed by reporters when writing a news story.

One of the first things you learn as a journalism student is the Five Ws. I know you're probably ahead of me, but I'll say them anyway: "Who, What, Where, When, and Why." In journalism, the Five Ws represent five questions that, if asked correctly, will provide you with the essential information you need to write a good news story. "Who was shot?" "What were they doing at the time of the shooting?" "Where was the victim standing?" "When did the shooting take place?" "Why was the person shot?"

Before you can develop your messages, though, you need to have a good idea of the questions you'll likely be asked by whomever will be asking the questions. That's where the Five Ws come in.

Of course, you can ask many different questions using the Five Ws, but the fact is if you stick to these questions, you'll eventually get the information you need. If you don't believe me, go back and watch *All the President's Men*. Not only is it a very entertaining movie, it's one of the best examples you'll ever see of somebody using the Five Ws to gather information. In case you don't remember, the "somebodies" were *Washington Post* reporters Bob Woodward and Carl Bernstein who were hot on the trail of the political story of the century and were featured not too long ago on every television talk program in America with the revelation of the identity of "Deep Throat." Believe me, it worked for them—it'll work for you.

Before you can develop your messages, though, you need to have a good idea of the questions you'll likely be asked by whomever will be asking the questions. That's where the Five Ws come in.

Ask yourself the questions you would ask if you were asking the questions. Huh? Let me give you an example.

Let's say you were going to the bank for a business loan. If you were the banker, what questions would you ask? "So, Mr. Smith, what do you plan to do with the money?" "Why do you need a loan from our bank?" "Who exactly will be responsible for paying the loan back?" "Where do you plan to get your customers?" "When do you think you'll make a profit so you'll be able to pay back the loan in full?"

Once you've run through the Five Ws a couple of times, you should have a pretty good idea of what to expect when you sit down across from the no-nonsense loan officer. You'll also be able to determine what messages you'll need to deliver in order to secure that all-important loan.

But let's face it, some questions are more important than others. While the question, "Where do you plan to get your customers?" may be important, it's not half as important as the question, "What do you plan to do with the money?" Once you've reviewed the Five Ws, it's up to you to figure out which questions will be most important to your "audience." I trust, however, that you're smart enough to figure that out. After all, you were smart enough to recognize your need to improve the way you answer questions. Even so, let me share some tips with you for crafting messages that work.

Developing Three Messages That Matter

Once you've identified the questions you're likely to be asked by the person or persons asking the questions, you're ready to develop messages that address them. In my earlier example, I told you I expected my prospective employer to ask me about my job history. It made sense because that's exactly the question I would have asked. Having determined I would likely be quizzed on my employment record, I crafted one of my three messages to address this concern. But, keep in mind what we've already learned. Messages are more than answers to questions. They are key thoughts you want your listener to remember.

You can develop three strong, effective messages for just about any situation by answering the questions, "What," "How," and "Why."

That being said, I've learned an important thing about messages I'd like to share with you. If you are inclined to use a highlighter when you read but haven't thus far, this is the place to break it out. What I've learned is this: You can develop three strong, effective messages for just about any situation by answering the questions, "What," "How," and "Why." That's because the answers to these questions usually get to the heart of what you want to say about yourself, your product, or your company.

Think of it this way. If you were asked to walk onto a stage and to briefly describe for an audience the three most important things about your professional career, what would they be? My guess is, you'd probably tell them about WHAT you've done, HOW you did it, and WHY it's important.

Here's another way to look at it. When I was a senior executive working in high-tech public relations in Seattle before the technology bubble burst, we advised our high-flying clients to develop a good "elevator pitch." I suspect you've probably heard this term before. We worked with our clients to develop three messages about their companies they could deliver in less time than it took an elevator to descend five or six floors. Why? Since the lifeblood of many technology companies was publicity, it was essential for senior executives to quickly describe their companies in a way that would capture the interest of influential technology reporters and, hopefully, lead to stories about their offerings. And in those wild and woolly days, a CEO never knew when he or she might be riding in an elevator with a venture capitalist capable of writing a ten-million dollar check if they could interest them in their company by the time they reached the lobby. Without question, the fastest way to the lobby and the possibility of that ten million dollars was through good messages based on the questions "What," "How," and "Why."

So, even though I told you earlier to use all of the Five Ws to anticipate questions you may face in a meeting or an interview, I encourage you to make the questions "What," "How," and "Why" the focal point of your messages. While the questions of "Where" and "When" are useful in providing valuable detail, they need to take a back seat to the "Big Three" . . . "What," "How," and "Why."

Of course, in everything, there's an exception to the rule. While the Five Ws will be extremely helpful in anticipating questions you may be asked, don't get hung up focusing exclusively on what others might want to know. The real question is: What do YOU want THEM to know?

Remember when I asked the question, "Are you hungry?" While the answer was, "Yes," the message was, "I want ribs." Sometimes the information you want or need to deliver goes beyond the scope of a question, especially if it's something the other person hasn't thought of or doesn't know. And that's a perfect opportunity to deliver a message.

Let's say you're going into your annual perfor-

Every question is an opportunity to deliver a message you want to get across.

mance review. You and your boss both know you want and expect a raise. In fact, you know you'll probably get one. The only question is, how much? You want a lot; your boss wants to give you a little. When your boss asks you rhetorically why you've been out of the office so much this year, you acknowledge that your wife has been ill, but she's doing much better, thank you. Here's your message, something your boss probably doesn't know. "Even though I was out of the office attending to my wife's medical needs, I spent much of my time at home working on the Danielson project, which saved the company more than a million dollars," you say. Holy Grand Slam, Batman. What you've done is turn a very negative observation into a home run for the home team.

Keep in mind, though, the Danielson message was one of three based on the questions "What," "How," and "Why" you should have prepared in advance of the review. Whether you used the fact you saved a million dollars in response to a question about your time in the office or one about overall company productivity, the message about your contribution was the one you wanted and needed to deliver.

I can't say it enough. Every question is an opportunity to deliver a message you want to get across. We'll talk more about how to do that later in the book. Fortunately, though, most of the questions we answer in our daily lives don't require the kind of forethought needed for a performance review or a job interview. But the next time you'll be on the spot interviewing for a new job or seeking a raise, think about your messages and be ready to use them. Like that old TV commercial advised, "Don't leave home without them."

CHAPTER THREE

QUESTIONS THAT PACK A PUNCH

CHAPTER MESSAGES

What: Questioners often employ trick questions intended to trip you up, so you must be able to recognize these types of questions quickly in order to answer them effectively.

How: By using Loaded-Preface, What-If, A-or-B, and Third-Party questions, an experienced questioner can get you to say things you never intended to say or didn't mean.

Why: If you aren't able to identify questions intended to unnerve or trap you, you'll be at the mercy of a good questioner no matter how well you know your messages.

Even though most of the questions you'll face in the course of an interview, performance review, or business transaction will be one of the Five Ws (Who, What, Where, When, and Why), you need to be aware of the various types of stealth questions lurking out there. If that sounds slightly menacing, it's meant to. In addition to keeping you engrossed in my prose, it's intended to alert you to the fact that all is not fair in love and war AND in interrogations of any sort.

Every so often, you come upon that rare breed of interviewer who has developed a devilish ability and desire to trip you up. "How can they do it?" I hear you cry. "I know my messages!" Of course you do, but these people are sly and cunning. They are armed with techniques for asking questions that go back to the dawn of time. Okay, that may be over-stated, but they do employ tricks for asking questions that I'm about to share with you. In fact, if there were an organization for people who ask questions, I'd be tossed out just the way magicians are for re-vealing their secrets of illusions with the public. Nevertheless, it's a small price to pay, and I'm willing to pay it. So ladies and gentlemen, step right up as I share with you the mysteries of the Tricky Question Types.

Open-Ended Questions

Sometimes the easiest questions are the hardest. "Come again," you may say. That's right, sometimes the easiest questions are the hardest because many people don't know how to answer broad, Open-Ended questions concisely on subjects about which they know a lot. If you ask some executives to tell you about their companies, you may want to hunker down with snacks and a good book because you could be there a while. They're likely to "start at the very beginning," as advised in *The Sound of Music.* The last time I checked, however, *The Sound of Music* wasn't on the required reading lists for most graduate-level business communications courses.

Executives often start at the beginning because they believe that's what the person asking the question wants. Wrong. "So Mr. Johnson, tell me about your company." The funny thing about Open-Ended questions is they aren't really questions at all. They are actually invitations to talk about what you think is important. Unfortunately, many linear thinkers, and this includes an awful lot of CEOs I've known over the years, unintention-

For those who haven't thought through their messages, Open-Ended questions can be totally baffling because they don't know where in the vast ocean of their knowledge to dive in and, more importantly, where to climb out.

ally follow the advice of Julie Andrews. "Well," they begin, "we started the company in Houston in 1988 and moved to Dallas in 1992. By then we'd increased our number of employees from six to ninety-eight." I really hope you brought that book because it's likely to take some time for this executive to get around to telling you what his company actually does and why it's important. Clearly, he lacks an elevator pitch.

Again, if you don't know what you want to say, you can't say it. For those who haven't thought through their messages, Open-Ended questions can be totally baffling because they don't know where in the vast ocean of their knowledge to dive in and, more importantly, where to climb out. So they talk . . . and . . . talk . . .

I call this the "Blue Book" approach to communications. If you went back and examined the essay exams of these executives in college, I suspect you'd find they incorporated the same approach. Write down as much as you know, including every fact you can remember, and that will surely indicate to your professor how well you know the subject. And this worked for many of us, me included. Unfortunately, it doesn't work quite as well in the real world where decisions are often made in minutes, and most people operate in a constant state of information overload.

When I'm coaching executives on how to answer Open-Ended questions, I challenge them with this example:

> "I've got good news and bad news," I tell them. "We've booked you into Carnegie Hall to speak in front of every reporter, columnist, legislator, industry leader, and influencer in the country who would possibly have an interest in your company, product, or issue. That's the good news. The bad news," I say, "is the microphone will be on for only thirty-five seconds. What do you want to tell them?"

As I watch eyes dart back and forth and brows furrow, I explain that they don't have to and can't possibly say everything they know in thirty-five seconds. And the same is true when answering Open-Ended questions. When given the opportunity to say whatever you want, whether in front of a microphone or in response to an Open-Ended question, this is your chance to say what is most important—and what is important is contained in your What, How, and Why messages.

While Open-Ended questions often appear at the beginning of conversations, they can arise at any time. If you have prepared your messages and practiced them, you'll be just as effective at answering Open-Ended questions at the end of a conversation as you are at the beginning.

Examples of Open-Ended Questions

- "Could you please tell me about your company?"
- "Why do you think you'd be good at this job?"
- "Why should someone attend this conference?"

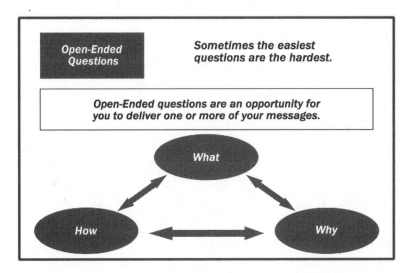

Many interviewers will begin and/or end an interview with an Open-Ended question, providing you an excellent opportunity to deliver one or more of your three key messages in any order.

Loaded-Preface Questions

I know you've been asked Loaded-Preface questions many times. You simply may not have known what to call them. Like a good spitball pitcher loading up the ball before delivering it to the plate, devotees of Loaded-Preface questions load their questions with incorrect information or opinion and deliver them as fact. And like a good "spitter," a Loaded-Preface question appears to be going one way when it suddenly veers another way.

Let me give you an example. You're talking with your supervisor about next year's departmental budget. You want more; he's giving you less. When you push back, he reaches into his bag of tricks and pulls out a Loaded-Preface question. "Ron, your department has met its goals every year for the last five years despite a reduction in budget, and you've done it rather easily. How can we trim it this year to make a real difference to the bottom line?" Smooth, very, very smooth. What your boss has done is characterize the last five years in a way that diminishes the effect budget cuts have had on your organization while complimenting you AND focusing your attention on the upcoming year.

"So, what's the big deal?" you may be asking yourself. The big deal is, if you allow the statement or preface about the effects of budget cuts on your department to stand, your boss will naturally assume you agree with it. And if you agree with it, isn't it logical to think you would be able to cut the budget even more this year without any adverse effects?

As Jimmy Buffet is fond of pointing out, we human beings are a strange bunch. While I'm not a trained psychologist nor do I play one on TV, I have observed that we can convince ourselves of just about anything. If you don't believe me, how do you explain the fact that many of us think watching baseball on TV is enjoyable? Seriously, though, we seem to have a great capacity to believe what we want to believe especially when we state things as fact and no one disagrees with us. Isn't that the basis of the "Big Lie?" If you repeat a lie over and over and over again, it will eventually become fact. That's what makes a Loaded-Preface question so powerful and dangerous. It reflects the bias of the person asking the question, so it mustn't go unchallenged.

That's what makes a Loaded-Preface question so powerful and dangerous. It reflects the bias of the person asking the question, so it mustn't go unchallenged.

In the example above, the boss WANTS to believe you cut the budget every year without effort. Hah! Has he forgotten you've lost several key people because they didn't get the raises they deserved? Has he forgotten that you've had to make do with out-of-date equipment because you don't have the money to replace it? Has he forgotten that everyone in the department is working longer hours because you haven't been able to fill vacant slots? Probably not. He's probably not an evil person, but he's got a job to do too. And the first thing he's got to do is convince you that it's no big deal to reduce what remains of your already inadequate budget.

That's why you must identify the Loaded-Preface and address it before you answer his question. For example, you could say:

"Ed, I understand you may think we cut the budget without much difficulty, but that just isn't the case." After you go on for a while about the negative effects of cutting the budget, you finally address the question. "So, as far as your question about cutting the budget even more this year, I'm sure you can understand why that would be a very risky thing to do for the company."

While I would like to tell you that by addressing every Loaded-Preface question you are certain to get your way, we all know that's not the case. But if you're able to identify a Loaded-Preface question for what it is and to correct the record immediately, it will make it easier for you to make your case and to keep the discussion focused where it belongs . . . on the facts.

Examples of Loaded-Preface Questions

- "I understand your company has lost a number of important customers; should we expect significant layoffs at your company?"
- "We all know that changes in the marketplace are going to make your product unnecessary in the future; in light of this, how will your company position itself in the future?"
- "Senator, you're not going to win this presidential primary; I don't think you're going to come in second, and I doubt you'll finish third, given that, would it be enough for you to leave the state knowing you have the best personal reputation among the existing candidates?"

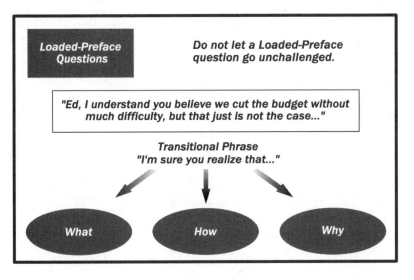

Loaded-Preface Questions

Do not let a Loaded-Preface question go unchallenged.

"Ed, I understand you believe we cut the budget without much difficulty, but that just is not the case..."

Transitional Phrase
"I'm sure you realize that..."

What   How   Why

What-If Questions (Speculative)

Sometimes referred to as speculative questions, What-If questions require you to peer into the future without the benefit of a crystal ball. Unfortunately, most of us are not particularly adept at regularly predicting what will happen tomorrow, much less next quarter or next year. If you are, what are you doing reading this book? I can think of about . . . oh . . . a million companies, many of them on Wall Street, that would like you to give them a call as soon as possible.

But just because you're not the Great Karnak doesn't mean people won't routinely ask you for predictions anyway.

But just because you're not the Great Karnak doesn't mean people won't routinely ask you for predictions anyway. "So, Mr. Jones, what are we supposed to do if our biggest supplier goes out of business next year?" How would Jones know, it hasn't happened yet? What Jones will or won't do, if and when that happens, will depend on many things. Are there new suppliers in the marketplace? Could several smaller suppliers take up the slack? Is the loss of the largest supplier actually an opportunity for the company? Circumstances dictate response. If you don't know the circumstances, how can you respond? You can't, at least not well. That's why it's important to recognize a What-If question quickly, to call it what it is, and to send it packing.

"But what's a little harmless speculation ever done to anyone?" you ask. If you're a fan of musicals, I remind you of the creative use to which Professor Harold Hill put speculation involving a "pool table" in Meredith Willson's, *The Music Man*. Without as much as a single fact or one piece of hard evidence, Professor Hill whipped the good people of River City, Iowa, into a frenzy over the evils of a pool table in their community.

He used speculation as misdirection. Misdirection, by the way, is what makes magic . . . well . . . magical. A magician is able to make a car disappear because you're busy watching his pretty assistant. It focuses you on the wrong thing. And while misdirection certainly has its place on stage, it has no place in a serious discourse. Don't get drawn into answering these kinds of questions. You'll eventually regret it. Why? What was that old potato chip line? "Bet you can't eat just one." People who ask What-If questions can't ask just one. Once they start you down the road to speculation, they'll keep asking and asking and asking. And you know what— you're not required to answer them.

If you ever watch the Sunday morning TV talk fests, you may have noticed that when a well-known politico is asked a What-If question, he or she will invariably say, "Well, I'm not going to speculate on that [*insert the name of your least favorite interviewer here*]." Did you ever notice how quickly the interviewer backs off? It's almost like holding a cross up to a vampire. And, yes, I am suggesting some of these interviewers are bloodsuckers. But you have to admit, as soon as the "S" word comes out, these otherwise aggressive defenders of the public good back off quickly. That's because there's a common understanding between interviewers and victims, sorry I mean interviewees, that it's perfectly okay to dismiss a speculative question out of hand. So if they can do it, so can you.

And here's the ever-present catch. If you start answering What-If questions, it's very difficult to stop suddenly when you want to. It's a little like asking a vampire to leave after you've invited him in. Your best bet is to say gently that you won't answer a speculative question and then stick to your guns. Sometimes, however, the first What-If question you're asked is one you're sorely tempted to answer because it works to your advantage. Resist. Say "No" to the speculation devil. Why? Because once you've answered one or two What-If questions that work in your favor, it's pretty hard to say you won't speculate on one that makes you uncomfortable. It's a little like taking the Fifth before Congress. Once you answer a single question, you're required to answer all of them. As your counsel, I strongly suggest you take my advice on this. Don't answer even one What-If question because, as I'm here to testify, the road to hell is paved not only with good intentions but also with the answers to speculative questions.

Examples of What-If (Speculative) Questions

- "What will your company do if your workers go on strike?"
- "What would happen if an airplane flew into the Sears Tower?"
- "We expect the next poll to show you leading in this election, how will that impact your campaign?"

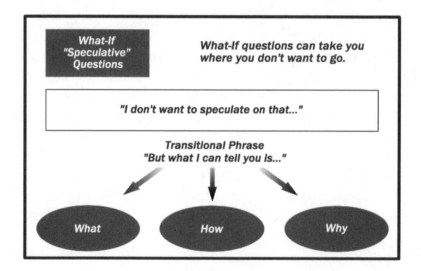

A-or-B Questions

If you're at all like me, you grew up watching your share of game shows, at least when you stayed home from school. I especially liked the one where you had to pick what was behind Door Number One, Door Number Two, or Door Number Three. Very simple, one, two, or three? Okay, pick one.

But as I grew older, I learned something pretty important. Sometimes there are choices other than those offered to you, especially by a game-show host. Unfortunately, many people out there would like to limit your choices, make you play by their rules. Not surprisingly, these people often frame their questions in ways that limit your answers to one or two choices. "Okay, do you want the Mercedes or the Kia?" "Wait just a gall-darn minute. What happened to everything in between?" These are called "A-or-B" questions and, regrettably, they often force you to choose between extremes, between black and white when you know most things are some shade of gray.

A-or-B questions rarely elicit serious answers because they are not serious questions, unless they're from the IRS. When someone asks you one of these troubling questions, they are actually trying to lead you to a conclusion by helping you answer the question. Why else would they give you two choices to pick from when there's a whole world of answers out there? Frankly, I find this rather rude.

That's why when you come face-to-face with a wily A-or-B question, throw off the shackles of convention and avoid answering it directly. But keep in mind, just because the person asking the question would like to help you answer it, doesn't necessarily mean the substance of the question is completely without merit. Go ahead and answer it, but answer it the way YOU want to answer it . . . with your messages. Ignore choices A or B and go directly to C, D, E, or F. It's a free country, at least it was the last time I checked. And while the Constitution may not specifically state you have the right to ignore the choices offered you in A-or-B questions, I have a sneaking suspicion the Founding Fathers would have been very sympathetic to this cause.

Examples of A-or-B Questions

- "Do you think the Redskins or the Cowboys will win the division this year?"
- "Will your company grow significantly or shrink dramatically in the next five years?"
- "Would you rather have a salary or work on full commission?

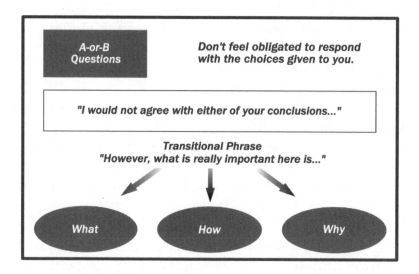

Third-Party Questions

"If you don't have something good to say about someone, don't say anything at all." How many wars could have been avoided if a few more people had followed this simple advice our mothers gave us? Regrettably, speaking poorly of others has become a contact sport in many places, not to mention the workplace. Stop and think for a moment. How many unkind things did you hear today about a co-worker, a customer, or someone at your company?

If you think I plan on giving a sermon on workplace etiquette, you're wrong. Bash away all you want. We're talking practical office politics here. You see, there's a type of question some people ask when they want to throw you off your game or simply to whip up trouble. It's called a "Third-Party" question. This is how the game is played.

You're answering questions quite effectively, relying on the techniques you're learning in this book, when out of the blue your interlocutor says something like, "Oh, and did you know that Peters over in marketing said, 'You don't know your (bleep) from a (bleep)!' What do you think about that?"

My, my . . . you never did like Peters very much. In fact, you've always considered him one step up the evolutionary ladder from a snake. So, about this time your face flushes, your heart rate accelerates, and your mouth goes into gear. "Let me tell you what I think of Peters. (Bleep) (Bleep) (Bleep) and (Bleep)!" Well, he started it, didn't he? Or did he?

When your blood pressure comes down enough for you to see clearly again, it may dawn on you that you never actually heard Peters say anything bad about you. You've taken another person's word for it, someone who may or may not have something to gain from open warfare between you and your reptilian colleague, someone who can't wait to tell Peters and everyone else in the company what you said about him. Maybe Peters said no such thing. Furthermore, you've likely made a serious mistake by acting in a very unprofessional manner. Perhaps the person asking the question was simply trying to throw you off balance. Guess what? It worked. If you responded this way in front of your boss, it could definitely be a career-limiting move.

That's why it's a good rule never to respond to

a Third-Party question in a negative fashion. Think of it this way, if you didn't hear it, it didn't happen. Your best bet is to take the high road, or at least the middle road. Consider something noncommittal, such as: "You know, I've known Peters for a long time, and I've never heard him say anything like that. While we have had our professional disagreements on occasion, I respect his abilities."

Okay, you may have to swallow hard when you say that last part, but trust me, it will serve you well. Besides making you look extraordinarily poised and professional, it may have the unintended consequence of helping you overcome your differences with your rival.

If you're able to recognize the types of questions asked of you, you'll be in a much better position to answer them effectively. But keep in mind, most of the questions you'll be asked will be very straightforward and can be answered effectively with the messages you've thought about and prepared in advance.

Examples of Third-Party Questions

- "Bob Jones at the Chamber of Commerce tells me your company is in serious trouble and has little chance of success, how do you respond to that?"
- "Mike Smith of Local 697 says your company has refused to bargain in good faith, is that true?"

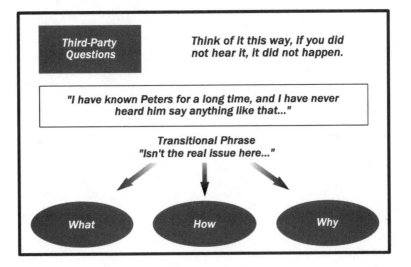

CHAPTER FOUR

MESSAGE BRIDGING: FROM ANSWERS TO MESSAGES

CHAPTER MESSAGES

What: A message bridge allows you to transition from the answer to a specific question, to one or more of your key messages.

How: By employing Transitional Phrases you're comfortable with, you can answer or avoid a question by bridging back to your messages as the focus of your response.

Why: A message bridge helps you transition from an answer back to your key messages and also helps you gracefully respond to questions you don't want to answer or are unable to answer.

Up to this point, I've talked about the importance of developing messages that help you communicate what you want to emphasize when answering questions. I've also showed you how to identify a few Tricky Question Types that could give you trouble. And while all of this may be enlightening, what good does it do you? I'm glad you asked, really I am, because it's time to answer that question. More importantly, it's time to show you how to use your messages to answer any kind of question from the simplest inquiry to the most complex interrogatory using a technique I call "Message Bridging." As its name implies, Message Bridging helps you cross the deep divide between the answer to a question and the messages you want to communicate.

The Direct Approach

The fact is, many times you can answer a question directly with one of your three messages. Neat and clean and no caffeine. "Why do you think you're right for this job?" It would be my hope that, after having read this book, you would hit this question so far out of the park that the ball would keep going for a day or two. Indeed, with a hanging curve ball like this, you should easily be able to deliver all three of your messages in response to this Open-Ended question. If you're prepared for it, it's very easy to answer, but, if you're not, it could be a swing and a miss. Having developed your three messages and practiced them before the interview, you're ready to answer this type of question to your fullest advantage. Indeed, no bridging is necessary because the messages themselves provide the answer to the question.

Locating Your Bridge

But sometimes when you're asked a question, there seems to be little or no way to reach your messages. Ah, but fortunately there is. Remember, every answer is composed of two parts, the answer itself and the message you want to deliver. It's simply a matter of crossing the bridge to the appropriate message. "Yeah, yeah, you've said that but HOW do I get to the bridge?" You use the magic words. And I don't mean "please" or "thank you." The magic words are called "Transitional Phrases," a few simple words strung together that help you cross over from answering a question to delivering your messages.

Remember, every question is composed of two parts, the answer itself and the message you want to deliver. It's simply a matter of crossing the bridge to the appropriate message.

Let me give you an example. You are interviewing for a manager's position at a local bank. You've worked for several banks and have extensive experience. This experience is one of your key messages.

After answering a couple of general questions relying solely on your messages, you are asked a question requiring more than a message alone. "So, you do seem qualified for the job, what salary are you looking for?" Ouch, the dreaded salary question. While salary is not one of your three messages, you should have prepared for this question, as should all job applicants. There are many opinions about how to respond to questions related to salary. In this case, I would suggest you bridge from your answer about salary to your message about your experience.

"Mr. Smith, the advertisement for the position indicated a salary between $45,000 and $55,000. In light of my experience, I think it would be appropriate for me to receive the upper end of the salary range."

Okay . . . this is where you could use a Transitional Phrase, such as, "As we discussed earlier . . ." to bridge from your answer about salary to your message about your experience in the financial world. It's this message about your experience that supports your argument for the higher salary, and, more importantly, moves the conversation away from a subject that may not be appropriate at this stage of the interview process. This is not a salary negotiation. You have not been offered the job. You have been asked a question about what you want for a salary, and it's probably in your best interest to move away from this subject as quickly as possible. And you would have done so very effectively by using the Transitional Phrase, "As we discussed earlier," to bridge to one of your messages. If this seems pretty simple, that's because it is. That's what makes this technique so powerful. You can use if over and over and over again with minimal preparation except for creating and practicing your messages.

Let's try another example. Let's say you're making a presentation to the board of directors of your company about increasing your advertising budget. You've thought through your messages, and you're ready to use them. You answer the first couple of Open-Ended questions easily, relying on the messages you've prepared. Eventually, the directors begin to drill down on the subject. "You're proposing we spend nearly ten million dollars to support our brand more effectively. Couldn't we rely more heavily on media relations to accomplish the same thing at a lower cost?" A very good question. Unfortunately, this question cannot be addressed directly using your messages, one of which is that strong brand recognition is developed through the consistent use of images and language communicated frequently to the public.

I would suggest you answer the question something like this. "Media coverage is very helpful in developing strong brand identity, no doubt about it. That's why we rely on it heavily to help tell our story. But that simply isn't enough because we can't control what's said about us or how it is said." You have answered the question but now need to bridge to your message. By using a Transitional Phrase, you can do just that.

"I think it's important to remember that . . . in order to develop strong brand identity, it's necessary for us to use the same images and language when we communicate with our customers, and that can only be assured through effective paid advertising." The Transitional Phrase, "I think it's important to remember that . . ." provided you with a safe and secure bridge back to your key message about the need for consistency in the brand messages the public receives.

Bridge Over the Question "Why"

We all have our own way of speaking. To a large extent, we are each a product of where we came from and how we grew up. While I'm a firm believer that you can improve the way you speak, I doubt seriously the average person has the time, energy, or drive to change their speech completely. And why would they want to? It's very much a part of who they are. That's why it's important for you to think about the way you speak and then figure out what types of Transitional Phrases you are most comfortable with. And these phrases need to fit you just as well as your favorite pair of jeans.

Since we all speak differently, it would be very difficult to offer suggestions for everyone. But think about the way you speak. Are there phrases you naturally use when changing the subject of a conversation? Here are some examples of typical Transitional Phrases: "That may be true, but I think what's really important here is . . ."; or "I understand what you're saying, but what I think our customers really want to know is . . ."; or "I see what you mean, but the real point here is . . ."

As long as the phrase you use makes sense in the context of the conversation, it really doesn't matter what words you choose to bridge to your messages. What does matter, however, is that you identify those phrases that work for you and that you begin to use them consciously. With some thought and a little practice, you'll find yourself transitioning from the answers to messages so seamlessly you'll probably surprise yourself with your newfound skill.

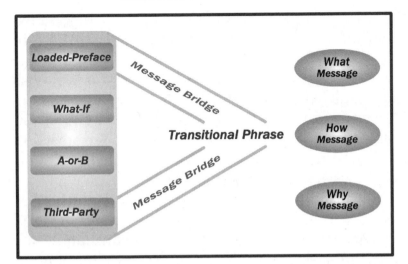

Examples of typical Transitional Phrases include: "But I think the real point here is . . .," "What's really important, though, is . . .," and "But what we should be focusing on is . . ." Transitional Phrases allow you to bridge naturally from a tricky question to your appropriate message or messages.

To Thine Own Self Be True

This is the part of the book where I should probably say a word or two about telling the truth. Since I'm not a clergyman, I have no intention of discussing the ethical or moral ramifications of falsehoods. But since I used to be a political reporter, allow me to deal with the very practical consequences of lying.

Unfortunately, the public landscape is littered with people who thought they could lie skillfully and get away with it. You don't need to look very

You don't need to look very far beyond recent headlines to find some good examples of what happens when you're caught "stretching" the truth or making it up out of whole cloth.

far beyond recent headlines to find some good examples of what happens when you're caught "stretching" the truth or making it up out of whole cloth. If you don't take my word for it, you may wish to speak with the short-lived coach of the Notre Dame football team who was ousted for embellishing his resume or the former CFO of Enron who's serving time in federal prison for embellishing his company's profit/loss statements.

The reason I bring this up is this. The technique I'm describing can help make you a very powerful and persuasive speaker, one who can handle the toughest questions with aplomb after a bit of practice. In my experience working with corporate CEOs, politicians, and other accomplished individuals, I've learned the best policy when it comes to answering questions is to answer them honestly and not to rely on any technique to intentionally mislead someone.

Before you accuse me of excessive naiveté, I'm not suggesting you turn every question into a mea culpa. A job interview, for example, is not confession nor is it an interrogation. Well, not usually. You're under no obligation to provide every detail about your behavior all the way back to the third grade. But you are, fundamentally, expected to tell the truth. And, if you don't do it for moral reasons, at least do it for practical ones.

If you lie, there's a good chance you'll ultimately get caught. Is it really worth your credibility or your good name? It may seem like a good idea at the time, but not later when it lands you in front of a grand jury or on *The O'Reilly Factor*. So, whether the phrase "truth is the best policy" was thought up by a priest or by a political consultant, the fact remains, it's pretty good advice.

CHAPTER FIVE

FACING THE MEDIA

CHAPTER MESSAGES

What: Unless you have a lot of experience working with the media, rely on your organization's public relations professionals to help you respond to media inquiries.

How: Reporters have a variety of ways of encouraging people inexperienced in working with the media to say things they wouldn't normally say on the record. They may make you feel comfortable and then hit you with a controversial question or allow you to wander off message and then pepper you with a string of tough questions.

Why: If you consult with a public relations professional who understands the rules of working with the media, you're less likely to receive negative coverage of yourself or your company.

If it's unlikely you'll be expected to talk with the media in your present job, you may still benefit from this chapter. After all, it's not only the media who's trying to get you to "spill" information or get you to trip up on a question or two. And the media is now such a pervasive part of our lives—you may find it interesting to learn some of the tricks of the trade.

Like the weather, everyone seems to have an opinion about "the news." And most of it, I fear to say, isn't good. Since there are plenty of radio and TV commentators making a good living talking frequently about the subject, I'll refrain from joining the "Fair and Balanced" debate. But I would like to call your attention to the similarity between widespread criticism of news coverage and the criticism of political advertising. "What does one have to do with the other?" you may be wondering. A lot. Try this experiment. Ask you friends or family to describe the characteristics of a news story.

Because I ask this question in every media-coaching session I conduct, I believe I can predict with some accuracy the words you'll hear. These include: biased, sensational, violent, celebrity-focused, scandalous, trendy, informative, and timely. There are more I could list, but, in a word, most people describe news coverage as essentially "negative." That's interesting because it's the same word you hear over and over again when people describe political advertising. And yet, despite this expressed disdain for negative news and negative advertising, it goes "on and on and on," like the Energizer Bunny. And why is that?

Before I answer this question, I want to characterize my opinion for what it is, opinion. It's not based on the findings of thinkologists who've conducted extensive research, perhaps at the expense of taxpayers, but rather on my own observations from years of experience in-and-around politics and journalism. So, now that I've shared this disclaimer with you, I feel light, buoyant, and unencumbered enough to give you my answer. And the answer is . . . drumroll please . . . we get what we really want.

"No, say it isn't so." Yup, I'm afraid there's no other conclusion to draw. The truth is, if you're running a political campaign, especially against an incumbent, you have almost no chance of winning unless you "go negative." Candidates run negative political ads because the conventional wisdom is— they work. And, unfortunately, the same can be said of news coverage. "Go positive," and see how long you stay in business. Despite what we say publicly, the fact is we seem to read, listen to, and watch negative news and are persuaded by negative political advertisements.

If you're going to be interacting with reporters, you need to understand what motivates them. And what motivates them are the audiences they serve and the negative news these audiences desire.

Okay . . . all that being said, what does this have to do with us? If you're going to be interacting with reporters, you need to understand what motivates them. And what motivates them are the audiences they serve and the negative news these audiences desire. That's why you not only need to be on your toes when dealing with reporters, you also need to craft your messages in a way that will resonate with them.

I'm not suggesting for a moment that you try to sensationalize what you do. I am, however, suggesting you look for ways to play up the human impact of what your organization does and find ways to describe these activities as part of a larger, ongoing trend story in which the media are particularly interested, such as the environment, the economy, or education.

As I said earlier, I've spent a lot of time on both sides of the camera, having worked as a television reporter and anchor, as well as a corporate and political spokesman and executive media coach. Having fired tough questions at newsmakers and having had them fired at me, I have a pretty good idea of what to expect during an interview. Again, keep in mind that many of the techniques I've already shared with you were developed specifically for talking with the media. And, fortunately for us, the techniques that work on *Meet the Press* also work in everyday life.

Like it or not, some of us are called on from time to time to answer questions from reporters. This is especially true if you're a senior executive in a corporation or an association. Okay, just between us, weren't those first few interviews you gave a little nerve-racking? Come on, we're all friends here—of course they were. If you're anything like me, not only were you worried you might come across badly, you also feared for your job. "Oh my God, everyone will be watching, including my boss! What if I screw up?" It sounds like the first time many of us drove a car, except for the part about everyone watching.

While talking with reporters may never compete with the enjoyment of driving a high-performance automobile on the open road on a warm spring day, it need not be a traumatic experience either. In fact, it can be pretty exhilarating when you do it well.

And what does it take to do it well? Confidence. Okay, pop quiz. What builds confidence? (Hint: we covered this back in Chapter One). Give yourself an "A" if you answered, "preparation and practice." This includes developing effective messages, practicing them, reviewing your list of Tricky Question Types (Chapter Three), and honing your bridging skills (Chapter Four).

If you're using skills you've learned from this book, you should have no trouble answering an inquisitive reporter's questions successfully. In fact, you should not only be able to answer questions well, you should also be able to represent your company's point of view most convincingly. Bear in mind, an interview creates a symbiotic relationship between reporter and interviewee. If you agree to an interview, the reporter has the right to expect you to provide information about the subject being discussed, and you have the right to say positive things about your organization, assuming they are true. When that happens, everybody wins.

But there's a catch. There always is. No matter how well you answer a reporter's questions, no matter how effectively you dodge tricky questions, and no matter how smoothly you bridge to your messages, the reporter, or his or her editor or producer, ultimately has the final say in what is printed or broadcast. "What an injustice," we grumble as we consider canceling that newspaper that ends up in the driveway only half the time anyway. But as Mark Twain supposedly observed, "Don't pick a fight with anyone who buys ink by the barrel and paper by the ton." Of course, today, he probably would have added, "And hairspray by the gallon."

So, how do we right this imbalance? We don't.

"It ain't fair, but them's the rules." What we can do, however, is know as much as possible about how to influence the outcome of a story. And yes, you've come a long way toward doing just that by knowing your corporate messages and using Message Bridging. But a little insider information about what goes on before and after a media interview never hurts either, especially if it evens the odds some.

Since I've probably divulged one too many secrets already, I might as well go the rest of the way. But remember, it's just between us.

Never Participate in Your Own Hanging

Even though you have little control after an interview, you have plenty before. When a reporter calls or your public relations department professional comes knocking, you want to find out as much as you can about the interview before agreeing to do it. Not only does that mean the time and date of the interview, but also the purpose of the interview. You would be surprised by how many people agree to be interviewed with only the slightest idea of what's going to be discussed. It may be the reporter is interested in doing a "profile" on your CEO and would like you to "confirm just a few facts." In other words, he may be doing a hatchet job on your boss, and he'd like your active participation. That sounds like a good way to enhance your career, doesn't it?

When a reporter calls or your public relations department professional comes knocking, you want to find out as much as you can about the interview before agreeing to do it.

When you're asked to do an interview, you want to find out as much as you can about the story. A reporter isn't going to volunteer much information, so it's up to you to ask. "What's the story about?" "Who else are you talking to?" "What exactly do you want me to talk about?" You get the picture. Fortunately, most interviews are benign and pose no danger at all. But it only takes one to sidetrack a promising career.

Let me take a moment to say a word about an often maligned group of people. No, I'm not talking about reporters. I'm talking about your friendly public relations staff down the hall or up a few floors. While you may have little use for them most of the time, believe me, they can quickly become your best friends when the media call. More often than not, they'll be the ones bringing an interview request to you. But that's not always the case. Whether they do or not, my advice is to let them find out what the reporter wants. Also, let them find out what they can about the reporter's point of view. They deal with the media all the time and know how the game is played. These media specialists can keep you out of hot water and even make you look good. Listen to what they have to say and rely on their judgment.

I strongly recommend that you have a PR pro in your office or on the telephone when you do an interview. In the first place, they can verify what you said or didn't say if the story goes south. Secondly, they can set ground rules for the interview and make sure the reporter sticks to them. Let's say you agree up front to talk about your company's push into new markets but not about the conviction of your previous CFO. If the reporter brings up this touchy subject, it's better to have your PR person remind the reporter of the ground rules than to have you do it. If the reporter is going to get angry with anyone for foiling his plan, it might as well be the PR guy or gal who gets paid for it. You can sit there and flash a sympathetic smile implying, "Hey, I'd love to answer that, but what can I do? The PR guy won't let me." You remain on good terms with the reporter, and, hopefully, he'll remember that when he prepares his story.

Calcagni's Law of Executive Contact

While I don't consider myself a pessimist, my job has always been to worry about my client, boss, or company. I suppose that makes me an optimist who knows things will go wrong. And one thing that often goes wrong for some inexplicable reason is a reporter circumnavigating the elaborate telephone defense systems created to keep them and others away from top executives.

Maybe it has to do with chaos theory. Keep in mind that even though the only thing I know about chaos theory comes from watching *Jurassic Park*, I am fully aware of the chaos that can result when a reporter suddenly reaches some poor unsuspecting senior executive. And if that isn't bad enough, let me share with you what I call "Calcagni's Law of Executive Contact."

According to Calcagni's Law, "When an executive is unexpectedly contacted by a reporter, the executive's mind will be as far away from what the reporter wants to discuss as it can be." In other words, if the reporter wants to talk about employee retention, the executive's mind will be completely occupied with budget numbers. And if the reporter wants to talk about your company's latest marketing success, the executive will undoubtedly be working on next year's strategic plan. You get the picture.

When a reporter calls, you need to be ready with your messages and fully focused on the interview. "But it's the *Wall Street Journal*!" I don't care who it is. If you're not prepared, don't do the interview.

Before the tech bubble burst, I had some technology clients who were absolutely convinced that the only thing standing between them and a billion dollars were a couple of strategically placed stories in a few highly sought-after publications. By the way, many of these companies have since gone out of business, and it had nothing to do with a lack of media coverage. Remember, these were the same guys who spent millions of dollars hiring hundreds of employees they didn't need to prove they were "scalable." And believe me, if a reporter called, these would-be-billionaire execs would do an interview even if they were sound asleep.

So what should you do if you're called and you're fast asleep, even at your desk? The first thing you do is find out who is calling and tell them you'll call them back shortly. Explain that you're wrapping up a meeting or completing a task, and you'd be happy to get back to them in just a few minutes. "But it's the *Wall Street Journal*!" I don't care who it is. The fact that it's the *Wall Street Journal* is even more reason to say you'll call them back. Do you really want to speak with one of the nation's most prestigious business publications without knowing what the newspaper wants or what you want to say? Of course you don't.

After writing down the reporter's name and phone number, ask that nice young man or woman in the PR department to contact the reporter and find out what he wants. This does a couple of things. It gets the PR department involved and gives the PR pros a chance to verify that the reporter is who she or he says they are. Gosh, wouldn't it be funny if one of your competitors called up impersonating a reporter, and you gave them all sorts of competitive information? Something tells me you wouldn't be laughing as you packed up the personal belongings in your office after the hoax was revealed.

If you decide to grant an interview, review your messages. If you don't have any messages, develop some quickly or don't do the interview.

If you decide to grant an interview, review your messages. If you don't have any messages, develop some quickly or don't do the interview. Reviewing your messages will focus your mind on the subject at hand and bring it back from wherever it has been. A quick review of your messages also will remind you of the key points you want to emphasize during the interview. Since a call from the media can come at any time, a good idea is to keep your messages easily accessible in a personal planner or on your PDA or computer.

Oh, and one more thing. If you say you'll call the reporter back, do it. Why? If you ever want to be called again for a story by that news organization, it's in your best interest to follow through on your promise. And besides, "It could be the *Wall Street Journal*!"

A Reporter Is Not Your Pal

Do you remember watching Peter Falk as Lieutenant Columbo? "Gee, my wife used to love that show." He used to catch the bad guys by making them think he was harmless because he seemed like a well-intentioned bumbling fool. Ah, but he was cunning like a fox. "Hey, where'd you get that knife, my wife would just love one of those."

Not to put too fine a point on it (my thought, not the knife), Columbo had a technique that worked very well for him. Reporters often use similar techniques to develop trust and rapport with people they're going to interview.

I consider myself to be a pretty friendly fellow. Whenever I'd visit the office of someone I was about to interview, I'd spend several minutes asking them about the photos or mementos placed throughout their office. Besides the fact that I am genuinely interested in the trophies and souvenirs people keep in their offices, getting someone to talk about them was a good way to help an interview subject loosen up. It also showed my interest in them as a human being. You see, I knew that if I could make the subject comfortable and trust me because I was a friendly guy, I'd get a better interview. If they figured they had nothing to fear from me, it was more likely they'd be open and honest, and maybe offer some information they might not otherwise provide.

My guess is, there are probably as many techniques for dealing with interview subjects as there are reporters. Just don't be fooled by a reporter who seems to care about you, when what he really cares about is what you might say that will make his story better. And when the camera is off or the pencil is down, remember, everything you say can and will be used against you in a story, because like it or not, you are always on the record.

Beware the Post-Interview High

I've noticed something over the years I find absolutely fascinating. It's a phenomenon I call a "post-interview high." You've probably heard over and over again about something called a "runner's high." It's a proven fact that runners produce pleasure-enhancing endorphins when they run. Since I hate to run, I will never know this experience unless one day I'm chased for a long distance by a pack of reporters. Nevertheless, I have witnessed similar reactions among people who have just ended (or so they think) a high-pressure interview.

"So that must be a good thing?" Wrong. Unlike a runner who has only to consume a two-dollar bottle of water when he's done, your job is not finished. Not only is your job not complete, but you are also at your most vulnerable point in the interview.

Imagine preparing extensively for an interview and worrying about it for days or even weeks. The big day comes, and you square off with the reporter. You deliver your messages convincingly, avoid tricky questions skillfully, and bridge like a veteran politician, and then . . . it's over. You made it; you survived! What a rush. You're on top of the world. Your confidence has never been higher, and those post-interview endorphins are rushing through you like concert-ticket holders in search of festival seating.

I often wonder how many careers have been undone by these post-interview highs. You see, it's at this point following a formal interview that the reporter says something casually like, "Hey, I hear your CEO is a real pain in the butt to work for, is that true?" And you, being Master of the Universe at that moment, say something clever and expansive like, "Yes, he can be a pain to work with, but he's a bright guy with great vision."

Oops. And the funny thing is you probably never felt the knife go in with all those endorphins at play. But you'll feel it when the endorphins have long departed, and the quote is right there in black and white. My guess is, you'll feel a lot like Sally Field's character in the film *Malice*, who runs from doorstep to doorstep gathering up newspapers before her neighbors have a chance to read an unflattering story about her.

Never, but never, let your guard down around a reporter, especially at the end of an interview as you are contemplating your new status alongside Superman, Batman, and Spiderman!

"Mirror, Mirror on the Wall"

I'm going to share with you another Tricky Question Type. It's called a "Mirror" question. Because Mirror questions are only a factor in media interviews, I chose to leave it out of the earlier list of Tricky Question Types.

Have you ever noticed, if you call someone a name, they'll usually deny it, but often do so by repeating the accusation in a much louder voice? "You are a scoundrel," you may charge. I've always wanted to call someone a scoundrel, but what good would that do? They probably would be doubled over with laughter, completely unaffected by my stinging rebuke. Then again, it could lead to a duel with pistols at twenty paces.

Anyway, should the object of my ire take umbrage with my characterization, he would probably reply in a volume much louder than my own, "I am NOT a scoundrel!" I do so love that word. Granted, this exchange sounds quite childish and more suitable to the playground than to a serious disagreement between twenty-first-century adults.

Unfortunately, this type of exchange is much more common today than you might imagine. It's also played out in subtle ways over and over again in news coverage. "Congressman, did you cheat on your taxes?" "No, I did NOT cheat on my taxes," the Congressman responds indignantly, handing the reporter a nice juicy headline. "'I Did Not Cheat on My Taxes,' Congressman Asserts." What the Congressman might have considered saying was, "That is totally untrue, and the facts will bear me out on this . . . (Transitional Phrase) . . . But I'd like to add that . . ."

The fact is, you never want to repeat a charge, or even raise it yourself, unless you're prepared to see it in print or blaring from radios and televisions wherever you turn.

The fact is, you never want to repeat a charge, or even raise it yourself, unless you're prepared to see it in print or blaring from radios and televisions wherever you turn. That doesn't mean you don't deny an untrue allegation and do so vigorously. It simply means you refrain from repeating the reporter's words so they can't be attributed to you or recorded for posterity.

Interestingly, this type of situation can arise during an interview that is not the least bit hostile and may be quite cordial and professional. In fact, potentially dangerous questions may even appear to be routine. "So, Bob, your company appears to be in tough shape financially, doesn't it?" In some ways, this is very much like a Loaded-Preface question. Assuming your company isn't in bad shape, you want to correct this perception immediately. But you want to do so without making matters worse. What you don't want to do is repeat the reporter's words, "No, we are not in 'tough shape financially.'"

The reason for this is simple. As we already know, the media have the final say on what is written or broadcast. If a reporter wants to make more out of a story than is truly there (of course this never happens), an easy way to do this is by quoting the words you used to disagree with his allegation.

And, as they say in Hollywood, at least I think they say it in Hollywood, this is where the magic happens. It's all in the writing. Let's say up to this point in a profile on your company the reporter has been describing how it began and grew into a market leader when suddenly he writes, "When asked about the company's financial outlook, president and CEO Robert James said, 'We are not in tough shape financially.'"

Okay . . . your words were taken out of context, but you did speak them. And let me remind you how many men and women have been led to the proverbial "gallows" proclaiming, "But it was out of context . . . It was out of context."

Regrettably, the phrase "out of context" has about as much credibility as the phrase "national security," when offered up as an excuse these days. You're always in a much stronger position when you can say, "I never said that," and mean it. And you're in an even better position if there was a PR pro in the room at the time of the interview to back you up.

I don't want to leave you with the impression that reporters are always out to get you, because they're not. But they are human, and like the rest of us, they sometimes make mistakes. My word of advice, however, is to do what insurance companies do. Reduce your exposure wherever you can. Provide one less opportunity for a reporter to make a mistake or to give in to temptation. Believe me, you will be misquoted, taken out of context, and generally abused from time to time if you interact with the media regularly. Over the years, I have observed the risk is generally worth the reward because most of the coverage you will receive will be positive and the value to your brand will be significant. But do everything you can to reduce the likelihood that you will be treated poorly. It's one thing to be the victim of bad reporting, but quite another to participate actively in your own hanging.

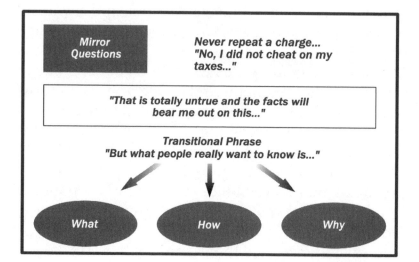

Making It Big on the Small Screen

Whether you're a company spokesperson or not, you may be asked to appear on television or radio as a content expert. More and more organizations are becoming aggressive in seeking what is called "earned media," as company leaders start realizing that free coverage in newspaper, magazine, and online articles—not to mention on television news programs and radio gabfests—is a much better way to get publicity than is paid advertising. Not only is earned media free, it carries the weight of an unbiased, third-party opinion. I've always believed, however, that this type of earned coverage has as much to do with a good PR campaign as it does with an organization's earned reputation as a leader in its respective industry.

If you're asked to do a radio or TV interview, you'll be expected to talk about what you know. Some people are experts on the impact of distraction on driver behavior, while others can speak authoritatively about the future of bio fuels. Some can even talk for days about the intricacies of model rocketry. Obviously, if you're asked to do an interview on TV or radio, you'll want to come across as knowledgeable and confident.

Because you're reading *Tough Questions—Good Answers,* you should be ready with key messages and prepared to take control of any of these interviews. Unfortunately, radio and TV interviews, especially live ones, come with their own special distractions. They also pose additional technical challenges that can make on-air interviews that much more daunting. Never fear, intrepid reader, your trusty guide is going to explain what you need to know to make your on-air experience a good one.

Television

Let's begin with television. Nothing can strike more fear into the hearts of many than the thought of speaking on television, especially live television. Unless you make your living at the business end of a camera or you're a public figure, such as a politician, a TV interview is a completely foreign experience. The words, "Toto, I don't think we're in Kansas anymore," come to mind.

Even those who have their messages down cold can be undone when the TV lights come on. Whoever said, "There's no substitute for experience," must have had television interviews in mind. There's a lot of truth to this, but, like everything else, it'll be a lot easier if you have a better sense of what to expect and how to act.

In the following chapter, I'm going to cover ways to help you appear more natural and relaxed during an interview or a Q&A session. In this chapter, however, I want to talk about some of the more technical aspects of interviews.

Before I begin, I want to remind you that everything you've learned up to this point about using messages and Transitional Phrases applies to radio and TV interviews, just as it does to print interviews or other situations in which you'll be responding to questions. If you don't know your messages, you have no business being in an interview at all.

Assuming you've thought through your messages and you're ready to use them, there are several things you need to know about TV interviews.

The number one question I am asked by those I've coached is, "Where do I look during the interview." Unless you are running for elective office or you are Ross Perot on *Larry King Live*, you look at the person asking you the questions. Think of the camera as eavesdropping on your conversation, the way another person might. This is especially true if you're being interviewed in a studio with multiple cameras. Your job is to answer questions, not keep track of which camera is on you at any given moment.

Unless you are running for elective office or you are Ross Perot on **Larry King Live,** *you look at the person asking you the questions. Think of the camera as eavesdropping on your conversation, the way another person might.*

I would, however, suggest that once you sit down for the interview, you always assume you are on, just as you assume everything you say is on the record. This is especially true if you are sharing the interview with another guest. You never know when the director is going to call for a reaction shot. The last thing you want to do is appear to be looking off into space or squirming in your seat.

More often than not, though, you're likely to be interviewed by a reporter at your office, standing up or sitting behind a desk or table. Again, focus on the reporter and let the camera eavesdrop.

If you're asked to do a live interview with a reporter or anchor in another city, state, or country who will be talking with you via satellite, you have no choice but to speak directly to the camera. These types of remote interviews are becoming more and more common and present a different kind of challenge. I believe that one of the most unnatural things in the world is to talk to an unfeeling, unresponsive, and unenthusiastic inanimate object, such as a camera lens. If you doubt me, pick out any object in your line of sight and begin talking to it about any subject you like. A word of warning—make sure there's no one around when you do. Don't stop for three minutes. My guess is you'll find it's a lot harder than you think. And I can assure you, it's about a hundred times harder than this when people are watching.

So how do you prepare for this kind of experience? That's easy. Develop your messages and practice, practice, practice with them as you would for any type of interview. I also recommend you rent or buy a video camera and tripod and have someone ask you questions off camera. Work on answering these questions as naturally as possible while speaking to the camera.

Don't be surprised to find that when you're finally seated in front of the camera during a satellite interview, you'll feel an overpowering need to break eye contact with the lens at some point. In my experience, this is very common and quite natural. How you do it, though, makes a big difference. Don't start looking around the room. This can, at best, give you the look of a trapped animal, and, at worst, make you look shifty and untrustworthy.

What are you supposed to do? Okay . . . pull out that highlighter again. My suggestion is—when you can't stand looking at that unrelenting eye one more second, simply glance down momentarily as though you are considering what you're saying and then resume eye contact with the lens. I don't know if Bill Kurtis, former CBS anchorman and host of *Investigative Reports* and *American Justice*, invented this technique, but he definitely turned it into an art form.

Another question I'm asked frequently is: "What should I wear?" This depends a lot on what you do and what industry you work in. It has become almost expected for a CEO in high tech to appear without a tie. For everyone else, it's a little harder to figure out. One thing you may want to do is find out how others have dressed during appearances in the past because you don't want to appear completely out of place. When I think about this, I'm immediately reminded of the photograph of President Richard Nixon strolling along a beach in a suit and dress shoes.

If you're a man, I don't think you can go wrong with a sport coat and tie. Why do I suddenly feel like I'm working at the Men's Wearhouse? Nevertheless, if you find a tie is inappropriate, you can always take it off and still appear stylish and authoritative. As for women, I recommend a blouse, blazer, and slacks. A former female colleague of mine once pointed out that you don't always know what kind of seating you'll find at an interview and slacks give women the greatest flexibility. I respectfully defer to her expertise on this matter.

I can, however, advise both men and women to avoid wearing intricate patterns and prints during television interviews. Not long ago, I tuned into a NASCAR race on TV in which former driver and commentator Darrell Waltrip was wearing a sport coat I could have sworn was alive. It appeared to be crawling all over him. I will spare you the technical reasons for this, but, suffice it to say, you don't want to wear anything, clothing or jewelry, that will distract viewers from what you are saying.

According to scientific research, most of us, with the possible exception of a few young actors and actresses in Hollywood, process a lot more information than just the words we hear when someone speaks. That's why we're able to listen to someone talking on TV while at the same time thinking to ourselves, "Man, that's the worst toupee I have ever seen," or "She's got to be in her sixties but doesn't look a day over forty. I wonder how many face-lifts she's had."

Even though you may be able to listen to what someone says and still make all those catty comments, you don't want people doing that to you. That's why I suggest women stay away from large brooches, intricate necklaces, and earrings the size of Hula-Hoops when on camera. Don't give people more reasons than they already have to become distracted while you're delivering your messages.

Radio

When it comes to radio, I have one point to make. Keep in mind radio is, fundamentally, entertainment. Even if you're appearing on what sounds like a fairly serious news-oriented program, chances are there's an entertainment program hidden beneath the covers. Rush Limbaugh . . . entertainment. Sean Hannity . . . entertainment . . . Laura Ingraham . . . that's right, entertainment. Don't get me wrong. These folks are very smart, they know the issues and they know how to entertain. Believe me, you don't get paid as much as they do for hosting a dull, public-service talk show.

So what does this mean for you? If you have the chance to appear on a local or national radio program, approach it with a sense of humor. That doesn't mean you can't seriously discuss your subject. You just need to be ready to mix it up good naturedly with the host or hosts.

A few years ago, I was doing a telephone interview with radio powerhouse WGN in Chicago. I was on the program to discuss AAA's Five Diamond hotel and restaurant award recipients that year. As I listened on the telephone to what was being broadcast, the on-air personalities began naming all the songs they could think of with the word "hotel" in the title. As I waited for them to get around to introducing me and the subject I was there to discuss, I heard the host say quickly something to the effect—"Tom Calcagni is with us from AAA to talk about the AAA Five Diamond Awards. Tom, what songs can you name?"

Fortunately, I had been paying attention to what was going on, unlike when I was in school, and had been thinking of additional song titles. Even though I was unable to contribute any new titles to the list, I was able to say I'd thought of "Heartbreak Hotel" and "Hotel California." This lighthearted banter led comfortably into the interview, which I would like to think came across as entertaining and informative to the audience.

CHAPTER SIX

STAND UP AND SAY IT

CHAPTER MESSAGES

What: You are more powerful and effective when you speak standing up.

How: Standing allows you to control your nervous energy and gives your voice more power.

Why: When you stand, you handle stress better and therefore perform at a higher level.

One of the realities of modern day life is the time we spend communicating by phone—mobile, wireless, and landline. And, while e-mail seems to be slowly, insidiously surpassing the spoken word as the communication vehicle of choice among harried business people, the King is not yet dead. Telephonic communication remains an important part of our lives.

From sales calls to radio talk-show appearances, the ability to answer questions effectively over the phone is as important as it's ever been, maybe even more so, as each of us has less and less time to accomplish the things we need to.

Speaking from personal experience, I much prefer answering questions when I can see the person asking them. In fact, I rely heavily on visual feedback to gauge if my messages are working.

Fortunately, the techniques you're learning in this book apply to any situation in which you'll be answering questions—whether sitting in your boss's office, squirming nervously in front of a loan officer, or taking a call from a local newspaper reporter. But let's face it, some situations are a lot easier than others.

Speaking from personal experience, I much prefer answering questions when I can see the person asking them. In fact, I rely heavily on visual feedback to gauge if my messages are working. I bet you do, too. It's quite natural to seek visual cues when talking with others and to respond to what you see. And that's the problem with the telephone . . . no visual feedback. You can't see that little raising of an eyebrow or that slight smile beginning to form.

So how do you respond when you can't see the person who is asking you questions? If you're like me, you get a little nervous. Some people get down right rattled. Neither is especially helpful if you're trying to make a good impression. So, short of finding a way to do the interview by video conference (forget putting your kids through college for what that will cost you), what do you do?

Stand up! "Excuse me?" You heard me. Stand up! "Why in the world would I do that?" It's quite simple, really. By standing up, you can get rid of some of the nervousness caused by launching your answers blindly into the darkness of telephonic space. Keep in mind, if you can't see who's asking the questions, they can't see you either. That means you are free to pace, gesticulate wildly, or do just about anything that makes you feel more relaxed.

I hail from a long line of leg wigglers. I'm sure you couldn't live without knowing that! But it's true. When my grandfather successfully ran for Governor of Vermont, he wiggled his leg so much that during campaign appearances, aides had to place a skirt around the bottom of any table at which he was seated so the audience wouldn't see his knee bouncing. And why did he wiggle his leg? I suspect it made him more comfortable in an uncomfortable situation.

Each and every one of us employs little tricks to relieve stress. So, whether you wiggle your leg like my grandfather, crack your knuckles, or bite your lip, the result is the same. You feel more relaxed. And from my experience with many different types of clients, the more relaxed you feel, the better you'll handle those tricky questions lurking just around the corner.

Standing Up for What You Believe

I don't want to leave you with the wrong impression that standing when you speak is only important when you're speaking on the phone. Quite the contrary. If you ask me, you should stand up any time you need to communicate something important. Obviously, you need to exercise judgment as to when this is appropriate or not. I guarantee you would get very strange looks from your colleagues if you kept popping up from a conference table like a jack-in-the-box every time you wanted to make a point. On the other hand, it would be perfectly natural for you to stand while presenting a report to your organization's board of directors.

Not only does standing when you speak allow you to relieve tension, it allows you to channel nervous energy into persuasive enthusiasm. Ask yourself, "Do I sound more energetic when I'm on my feet or when I'm sitting down?" Not surprisingly, most people agree, it's the former.

When I first started as a television reporter, I used to record the narration for my stories seated in a small recording booth. More often than not, I wouldn't be happy with what I'd recorded. It wasn't the words I had written, it was the way I was delivering them. They often sounded flat and boring. And I can tell you, flat and boring are not what you aspire to in local TV news.

I can't remember who suggested I stand up when I read my narrations, but it definitely wasn't my colleague who practiced primal screaming in his car and had little voice left to speak, let alone narrate. Whoever it was, I owe them a debt of gratitude. As soon as I was on my feet, there was more energy and power in my recordings. In a way, I'm surprised it took as long as it did for network anchors to get out from behind that anchor desk and onto their feet. Frankly, I think all of them come across much better this way.

Another reason it's better to speak standing than sitting is your voice has more power and resonance. I can't explain why this is true, only that I've been told that by choral directors, drama coaches, and on-air talent consultants. And it does seem to be true. If you want to sing well or to project your voice well, you need to use your diaphragm. You may have been in a chorus or choir at one time or another and probably remember that silly exercise in which you put your hand over your midsection and pant in order to feel the action of your diaphragm. It may not surprise you in the least to learn that your diaphragm can't do its job particularly well when you're sitting down, leaning forward, and squishing the air out of it. Suffice it to say, if this were the army, I'd be putting up signs exhorting you to "Be Good to Your Diaphragm and It'll Be Good to You."

When you stand, you not only allow your diaphragm to do its job, you also make yourself sound better and appear more in control. Not bad for an organ you know hardly anything about, is it?

CHAPTER SEVEN

MESSAGING FOR PRESENTATIONS

CHAPTER MESSAGES

What: Develop your messages for presentations the same way you would for an interview, keeping in mind time constraints and the information needs of your audience.

How: When developing presentation messages, think of your presentation as the answer to an Open-Ended question on the subject you're discussing.

Why: Not only will clearly defined messages help make your presentation more effective, but they also will prepare you for the inevitable questions that follow.

Let me ask you a question. Do you sometimes feel like your head might explode if you have to sit through one more PowerPoint presentation? I do. Unfortunately, presentations, especially those involving our favorite instructor, "Professor PowerPoint," are a way of life in the work-a-day world. But I am an idealist. I do not believe presentations have to be as mind numbing as Ben Stein's memorable character in the time-honored classic, *Ferris Bueller's Day Off.* "Bueller . . . Bueller . . ."

I'm pretty forgiving of most presenters, even those who are never going to make a living on the stage. But what I cannot forgive are presenters who don't know what they truly want to communicate and waste the time of their listeners. That should never be the case, and, after reading this book, I know you'll never make that mistake again, if you ever did in the first place.

Presentations offer a unique opportunity to use messages both during the presentation itself and during the inevitable question-and-answer session that follows.

Presentations offer a unique opportunity to use messages both during the presentation itself and during the inevitable question-and-answer session that follows. *Tough Questions—Good Answers* is not specifically written to prepare you for presentations. However, I would like to say a word or two about using messages to strengthen your presentations.

As I've said frequently throughout this book, you need to know what you want to say before you speak. The same is true when developing presentations. Craft your messages before putting mouse to pad. If you think about it, preparing for a presentation is a lot like getting ready for an interview where you expect Open-Ended questions. After all, isn't a presentation nothing more than the answer to an Open-Ended question? "So, Jill, what would you like us to know about your plans for next year?"

If you have thought through your What, How, and Why messages, you will know exactly what you want your presentation to communicate, and you will appear well prepared and knowledgeable. Of course, you also will need to add the level of detail required to satisfy your specific audience and conform to the time allotted. Good messages combined with appropriate detail make for good presentations. And the *piece de resistance* is you will be ready for whatever questions are thrown at you during the Q&A session afterward.

You'll also want to keep an eye out for questions that may not be "tricky" but which could pull you way off message.

You'll need to keep in mind the Tricky Question Types you've learned and watch out for them. You'll also want to keep an eye out for questions that may not be "tricky" but which could pull you way off message. It's not only professional interviewers who know how to launch interrogatory missiles. How many times have you heard someone ask an off-topic question following a presentation because the speaker didn't address what that person hoped they would? "Mr. Kleuver, I understand how your system works with large numbers of consumers, but in our business, we deal with large numbers of business buyers. Would you approach the development of a business-to-business call center the same way?"

It's a fair question, but one you're not prepared to answer. What to do? Your first instinct may be to take a stab at it to show you are helpful, responsive, and nice. Why not, you've been trained to do that since kindergarten? What you should be saying to yourself, however, is the line made famous by Dana Carvey in his send-up of former President George Herbert Walker Bush, "Not gonna do it."

While answering this particular question may not be your undoing the way Iraq has been for the second President George Bush, why take the chance of saying something inadvertently to undermine your credibility or take the focus off the messages you've worked so hard to prepare? Keep repeating it. "Not gonna do it." Hopefully, what you are gonna do is use a Transitional Phrase to bridge adeptly from this potentially sidetracking question to your messages. Employing your newfound skill, you could say something like, "Thank you for that question, and I would be delighted to speak with you about the topic after the meeting. I think what is important here though is . . ." Without putting your presentation at risk, you've demonstrated to your questioner and to the audience that you're helpful, responsive, and nice.

You are probably familiar with the advice that's been given to speakers for years to boost their confidence. Someone once suggested they imagine their audience naked. I never understood why, but for some reason, this approach gained wide currency. It never worked for me. Frankly, I prefer to look out over my audience fully confident I know what I want to say, equally confident my listeners know it too.

CHAPTER EIGHT

MESSAGING FOR THE WEB

CHAPTER MESSAGES

What: Messages matter to people, but words and context matter to search engines. Your Web presence will be more effective if you develop messages that communicate specifically to your target audiences.

How: By understanding the purpose of your online presence before building a site, you'll be able to deliver the right content to your audience whether they are consumers, business-to-business contacts, the media, and even search engines.

Why: Just as messages allow you to take control of any meeting, interview, or conversation, clear messages on your blog or website help to make your online presence more powerful and effective.

If you're a blogger or write for the Internet in one way or another, as millions of us do, you not only need to know your messages, but you also need to know how to communicate them quickly, clearly, and in an entertaining manner in a very dynamic environment. This was true before blogging, and it's even more so today.

With one-and-a-half blogs created every second of every day, the amount of editorial content on the Internet today is so vast that writers have precious little time to make an impression on the audiences they hope to reach. With time shrinking to research, read, and absorb information and the availability of online information growing astronomically, have you ever wondered what it really takes to make your Web writing stand out? What type of text grabs the attention of users increasingly strapped for time and faced with endless possibilities for content, not to mention advertising?

It may surprise you that Web communicators can learn a thing or two from an older, more traditional communications medium . . . television.

It may surprise you that Web communicators can learn a thing or two from an older, more traditional communications medium . . . television. And, more to the point, Web communicators can do a better job of expressing information and opinion by using the same messaging techniques presented in *Tough Questions—Good Answers.*

Television news writers, reporters, and editors discovered a long time ago the value of clear, crisp, economical prose to grab viewers quickly and not let go. While you can argue the need for this type of clarity and brevity was driven by the limited airtime allotted to news broadcasts in the years before 24-

hour-a-day cable news, I think there's an even simpler explanation. When you write for the ear, as you do in television and radio, you get one pass at your audience. If you think about it, even the 24-hour news channels continue to serve up provocative prose to prevent you from switching channels. Consider this: Is television viewing really that much different from surfing the Internet—viewing Web pages, listening to podcasts, or watching videos embedded in corporate websites selling the latest and greatest technologies?

Think of it this way. If, when reading the Sunday morning newspaper, you come across an article that doesn't seem to make sense, you can go back and read it again. But in the days before digital video recorders (DVRs), you couldn't just rewind and watch a TV news story over again. As a broadcast reporter, you knew you had only one shot at your viewer or listener so you needed to make it count. Even in today's world of DVRs and browser bookmarks, in which it's almost a snap to return to recorded programs or bookmarked websites at your leisure, how many of us actually revisit what is now an "old" story? And that, my friends, is the rub.

If you're like just about everyone else I know, you have less and less time to do business research or enjoy leisure time. Have you noticed how insidiously your workday has crept into what was once your personal time? Doesn't it sometimes feel like dropping off your shirts at the drycleaner has become a leisure activity compared to responding to business e-mail and text messages at all hours of the night and on weekends?

So let me ask you this. How often do you erase a recorded program without viewing it or return to a website that failed to hold your attention long enough to read or view it the first time around? If recording and failing to watch a TV program were a felony, I would be sentenced to life without the possibility of parole. Time and again, the programs I record for later viewing either delete themselves, as the time for saving them expires, or I delete them in favor of recording newer, more relevant programs. And my experience with websites isn't much different.

Because the online information I would like to read would probably take a lifetime or two to do so, I seldom return to sites I've bookmarked. If a website isn't worth perusing or a blog article worth reading when I find it, it probably isn't worth reading at all. Them's the facts. And the reality is, there are probably many more Web pages or blog articles containing similar if not the exact same information. And while I always suggest people beware of focus groups of one, I suspect my experience with saving TV programs and revisiting websites is not all that different from the average bear.

Developing messages for your website or blog is a lot like developing messages for an interview, presentation, or discussion with colleagues on setting next year's departmental objectives. Not surprisingly, my wife Liz, who was a former business manager at one of the early social networking sites, Classmates.com, and consults with companies on the development of websites, emphasizes the need for sound message development before design is even a twinkle in a developer's eye.

While this may seem obvious, you would be surprised how many companies want to discuss the intricacies of color and layout before they have any idea what they want to communicate about the company or its products or services. And to do so, according to Liz, is truly to put the cart before the horse.

So where should you begin in developing your messages for the Web? You guessed it. Begin with What, How, and Why—the same messages you'd use when interviewing for that high-salary Web marketing job. Whether you're designing a new corporate website or developing content for an existing one, you want to make sure your site, its navigation, and each specific content area reflect your key messages. Decide whom your target audiences are and communicate these messages as clearly and effectively as possible.

Ah, if it were only that simple. With the prominence search engines play today in ferreting out relevant information through organic searches, that's a high-tech term for results that aren't paid for when you do a search, your messages not only need to contain wording intended to impress human beings, but they also need to include words and phrases relevant to search engine algorithms. I was never very good at math and don't much like anything called a "search engine algorithm."

Bottom line, if you want other people to see what you've written or what you have to sell, you had better have the right wording in your messaging to ensure your website or blog will show up on the right search engines. To do this, you're going to want to get to know the developer down the hall in IT who works on your site to make sure he or she understands your messages as well as your management, designers, and writers do. So I suggest you plan on a significant line item in your budget for pizza because you are probably going to be spending an awful lot of time together in the weeks and months ahead.

CHAPTER NINE

CONCLUSION

*H*aving *learned how to craft* effective messages, identify Tricky Question Types, and successfully bridge from any question to your key messages, you're now ready to put these skills to good use. You may not be ready to run for the U.S. Senate yet, but then again, maybe you are. Fortunately, the techniques I've described are not difficult to master, but they're likely new and different to you. And, let's face it, many of us find it awkward and uncomfortable to try new things.

I can't tell you how many business books or how-to manuals I've read on various subjects and how many I've packed away without giving them a fair chance to make me a better business professional or a better human being. Why? It's not because I'm lazy. Well, at least I don't think I am. After all, I took the time to read those self-improvement books in the first place. No, I think it had more to do with the fact I was afraid I wouldn't do whatever it was I was encouraged to do, perfectly. So instead of giving it the old college try, I simply absorbed as much information as I could and swiftly moved on to the next best seller.

Why, you may ask, am I bearing my soul to you about this? They say confession is good for the soul. (So is a double caramel macchiato.) I simply don't want YOU to walk away from the valuable techniques in this book without giving them an honest-to-goodness test-drive.

And to make this as easy as possible for you, I've included a practice session in the following chapter. It will help you create your first set of messages and prepare you to use Transitional Phrases to bridge successfully from tricky questions to your messages.

In my role as a media coach, I've watched first-hand as numerous corporate CEOs, association executives, and published authors quickly became better communicators by using the techniques I've described in this book. And trust me, most of them weren't any better at this than you are when they began. But they WERE willing to try and their efforts paid off handsomely as they saw their communications skills improve markedly.

Okay, enough of the pep talk. Let's get practical. What do you have to lose? Even if you don't need to organize your life into ten-minute increments or figure out who moved the cheese, you do need to answer questions each and every day. So, you might as well be good at it, right?

When I work with clients, I usually explain that the more comfortable they are in any given situation, the better they will perform. Pretty obvious, isn't it? You're much more likely to be charming and witty sitting in your living room with close friends and family than you are stranded on the side of the road in the rain with a flat tire. If you think of these two real-life situations as opposite ends of a spectrum, every step you take from the car on the side of the road toward your friends and family in the living room makes you more comfortable and, no doubt, better company. The same can be said for answering questions. Everything you do to make yourself more comfortable when answering questions will help you answer them more effectively. It's really that simple.

And that's where the techniques in this book come in. If you can recognize tricky questions and bridge effectively to your key messages, you'll be more confident in your ability to handle the toughest questions anyone can throw at you.

If you don't know what you want to say, you can't say it effectively. What are the points you want to make and the points you want your listener to remember?

But remember, everything begins with good messages. If you don't know what you want to say, you can't say it effectively. What are the points you want to make and the points you want your listener to remember? By asking yourself the questions "What," "How," and "Why," you'll be able to develop strong messages you can emphasize over and over again for maximum impact.

But do yourself a favor, don't wait until right before a critical interview or board presentation to begin learning how to develop good messages. You wouldn't wait until the night before a company golf tournament to learn how to hit a golf ball would you? The more practice you get developing messages, the better you'll be at it when the chips are down and you really need them.

So, complete the "Preparation and Practice" exercises in Chapter Ten. These will help to strengthen your message development muscles. Focus on the everyday questions first. In other words, develop messages to answer the following basic questions: "What do you do for living?" "What are your hobbies?" "How would you describe your company?" And listen to the way you speak. Identify the Transitional Phrases you naturally use and begin using them to bridge from your answers to your messages.

Even if the questions above weren't that tricky, you might want to begin paying closer attention to questions you hear on TV or in meetings. As you learned earlier, messages are not only good for reinforcing important thoughts you want to leave with a questioner, but they also give you a way to handle tough questions intended to trip you up. Whether you are answering an Open-Ended question, a Loaded-Preface question, a What-If question, an A-or-B question, or a Third-Party question, it's important to address it as best you can and then bridge as quickly as possible to your key messages.

I simply can't say it enough. Messages are the cornerstone of successful communications. And with a little practice, you'll be surprised at how naturally you begin using them in your everyday life.

Not too long ago, I was media training a colleague of mine. After our initial session, I asked if he'd had a chance to use what he'd learned. What he said both surprised and delighted me. Not only do he and his wife watch the Sunday morning talk programs together to see how messages are used, but he also told me that when they're having a "discussion," one of them will sometimes say to the other, "You just used a message on me," prompting the other to reply, "No, you used a message on ME!"

Like it or not, each of us is called upon to answer questions every day. Many we can prepare for; many we cannot. But for those questions we know we're likely to face, doesn't it make sense to answer them the very best we can? I encourage you to use the techniques outlined in *Tough Questions— Good Answers*. And even though they may not help you grow more hair, they will make you a more successful communicator.

CHAPTER TEN

PRACTICE SESSION

If you've stayed with me this far, give yourself a warm pat on the back, and, if you're self-employed, what the heck, give yourself a raise, too. I've been telling you throughout *Tough Questions—Good Answers* that the techniques described in this book are easy to use. Frankly, the features on your mobile phone are more challenging, but that's probably not stopping you from snapping pictures with your built-in camera or surfing the Web with your mobile browser.

As I said in the previous chapter, you need to give these techniques a test-drive. If you're still hesitant, remember how hard it seemed when you first learned to ride a bike. I was scared to death, but not as scared as the old woman down the hill who stood frozen in her tracks as a shrieking five-year-old barreled toward her on a two-wheeler.

The exercises that follow are intended to jumpstart you as you begin developing personal or professional messages. Keep in mind, you can and should develop messages for all occasions and subject matter. For the purpose of these exercises, I think it would helpful to select one subject of current interest on which to focus. If you're getting ready for a job interview, you may want to consider your personal messages. If, on the other hand, you're in need of a corporate elevator pitch, you could focus on your corporate messages.

If you have questions or comments about your messages after completing these exercises, you can contact me via my website: www.toughquestions goodanswers.com.

Okay . . . enough talk. Let's start creating messages.

Preparation

Before you begin writing your What, How, and Why messages, you first need to identify which characteristics about your organization are significant and which ones you want to emphasize. (For the purposes of these exercises, we're going to work on developing messages about your company, firm, or organization. Feel free, however, to create personal messages instead.)

Please complete the following:

List the three most important services or products your company or organization offers.

1.

_____

_____

2.

_____

_____

3.

_____

_____

List three accomplishments or measures of suc-cess your organization has achieved in the past year.

1.

_____

_____

_____

2.

_____

_____

_____

3.

_____

_____

_____

List three things that differentiate your organization's products or services from your competition. (Keep in mind the audience you are focusing on.)

1. _____

_____

_____

2. _____

_____

_____

3. _____

_____

_____

List three "problem" areas or what others may see as your company's vulnerabilities (so you can anticipate questions about them and, if necessary, address them in your messages).

1.

_____

_____

_____

_____

_____

_____

2.

_____

_____

_____

_____

_____

_____

3.

_____

_____

_____

_____

_____

_____

Business Messages

Review your responses in the previous exercises. As you think about what your messages should be, remember that your messages need to communicate quickly and concisely the most important information about your company. You accomplish this by answering three questions: What, How, and Why?

● **What Message:**
(Example: The XYZ Company is the world's largest manufacturer of commercial corrugated boxes with operations in thirty-six countries and revenues in excess of $1 billion.)

_____

_____

_____

_____

_____

● **How Message:** (Provide some specifics.)

(Example: The XYZ Company provides low-cost, same-day shipping anywhere in the world, an easy-to-use catalog with more than 20,000 items, the industry's best customer service program, and an unconditional money-back guarantee.)

_____

_____

_____

_____

_____

● **Why Message:**

(Example: With operations in countries throughout the world, we are the best choice to meet the packaging needs of the smallest to the largest companies quickly and efficiently while ensuring the best quality and value anywhere around the globe.)

_____

_____

_____

_____

_____

Message Practice

Congratulations! You have created your first set of messages. If you have developed corporate messages, you now have a strong elevator pitch. And, if you have created personal messages, you should now be able to describe yourself powerfully and convincingly to a prospective employer.

Of course, you still need to use your messages. So, let's give them a spin, shall we? I have posed several straightforward questions for you to answer using your messages. Again, if you're working with personal messages, modify the questions for your use. For this exercise, practice speaking your messages aloud. Look at your written messages first, and then try to answer the following questions without peaking at your notes.

• What does your company do?

_____

_____

_____

_____

_____

● How would you describe your organization?

_____

_____

_____

_____

● What type of company do you work for?

_____

_____

_____

_____

Now that you have your first set of messages, see how often you can use them. But, as the late Crocodile Hunter Steve Irwin might have said, "Whoa, this is the really dangerous part."

You need to keep your messages top-of-mind and use them at every opportunity so they become almost second nature to you. Chances are you will have an opportunity to use them almost every day. Also, for extra credit, sit down and watch one of the numerous political talk shows on TV, one in which a host interviews guests. See if you can identify the guest's three messages. Believe me, they have them. How well they use them will be up to you to decide.

Feel free to continue the exercises or wait until you've become comfortable using your new messages. If, however, you think procrastination may rear its ugly head, then by all means, keep going!

Use of Transitional Phrases

If you have been practicing with your new messages, and even if you haven't, you are probably ready to begin using your messages to answer the Tricky Question Types I have outlined in Chapter Three.

Before you begin, however, you need to take a few minutes to identify Transitional Phrases you commonly use. Remember, these are important when you bridge from the answer to a tricky question to one of your messages. If you are unsure of what a Transitional Phrase is, review Chapter Four or simply think of a phrase you commonly use when you want to change the subject of conversation. Voila. That's a Transitional Phrase.

Write down three phrases that come easily and naturally to you when you want to transition from one subject to another. Take note over the next several weeks of Transitional Phrases you use frequently and add them to the list:

(Example: "What is really important, though, is . . ."

_____

_____

_____

_____

_____

Write down Transitional Phrases you notice others using:

_____

_____

_____

_____

_____

Tricky Question Types

Okay . . . you're almost ready to pull together all you've learned about answering tricky questions and taking control of any interview. But, before you take this next step, I want to test your ability to identify the types of tricky questions that could be thrown at you. By the way, everyone receives a passing grade. (Hint: You may, however, want to review Chapter Three, on Tricky Question Types, and Chapter Five, "Facing the Media," before you begin.) Please identify the following Tricky Question Types:

Question 1: Is your firm's greatest strength its clients or its personnel?
Answer:

_____

Question 2: What can you tell me about your company's marketing program?
Answer:

_____

Question 3: Your industry is clearly in a downward spiral; what type of financial changes are you planning for the next three years?
Answer:

_____

Question 4: A leader of the local union representing your workers told me your company isn't bargaining in good faith; how do you respond to that?

Answer:

_____

Question 5: Isn't it true your company is woefully out-of-step with the times when it comes to global climate change?
Answer:

_____

Question 6: What would happen to your organization if charitable giving dropped by 10 percent?
Answer:

_____

Message Bridging

With any luck (and the hint I gave you above), you were able to identify successfully the six Tricky Question Types. If so, go to the head of the class. If not, please take a few minutes to review the important Chapter Three on Tricky Questions Types again, as well as the "Mirror, Mirror on the Wall" section in Chapter Five. You need to understand these basic question types in order to take control of them.

Tricky Question Types Answers

1: A-or-B question; 2: Open-Ended question; 3: Loaded-Preface question; 4: Third-Party question; 5: Mirror question; 6: What-If (Speculative) question.

In this section, you are going to practice responding to tricky questions with an answer followed by a Transitional Phrase then bridging to your message(s). For those of you not as averse to math as I, the equation looks something like: Answer + Transitional Phrase + Message(s) = Control of a Question.

Since you already answered Open-Ended questions earlier when practicing your messages, and because they don't require a Transitional Phrase or Message Bridging, I have omitted an Open-Ended question from the practice list that follows. Please respond to the following questions, remembering to use a Transitional Phrase to bridge to your message(s). Since I don't know the specifics of your organization or industry, I'll need you to play along with the questions as though they apply to your company or marketplace.

LOADED-PREFACE QUESTION

- With globalization making it difficult for companies in your industry to compete, how does your company view the future?

_____

_____

_____

_____

_____

● Since new technologies are making products like yours obsolete, what is your marketing strategy for this year?

_____

_____

_____

_____

_____

● As more and more people are concluding that their charitable contributions are not being used wisely or for the purposes for which they were intended, what does your fundraising picture look like next year?

_____

_____

_____

_____

_____

WHAT-IF (SPECULATIVE) QUESTIONS

● What would your company do if a transportation strike shut down deliveries to your plants out West?

_____

_____

_____

_____

_____

● What do you think the effect would be of four-dollar-a-gallon gasoline prices on your business?

_____

_____

_____

_____

_____

● How would your company react to a possible hostile takeover bid?

_____

_____

_____

_____

_____

A-or-B Questions

● Do you think your organization would be hurt more by a dramatic spike in inflation or by a sudden downturn in the economy?

_____

_____

_____

_____

_____

● What do you think charitable organizations need to do to encourage increased giving—emphasize the tax breaks associated with charitable contributions or focus more on the needs of the disadvantaged?

_____

_____

_____

_____

_____

● Should Congress cap civil penalties against corporations or leave the issue completely in the hands of juries?

_____

_____

_____

_____

_____

THIRD-PARTY QUESTIONS

● I understand from a colleague in auditing services that your department has been acting outside commonly accepted accounting practices, how do you explain that?

_____

_____

_____

_____

_____

● Alderman Mary Smith tells me there is little chance your company will receive the permits it needs to expand your plant, what is your response?

_____

_____

_____

_____

● Officials at the union representing your employees say you plan to "lock them out," is that the case?

_____

_____

_____

_____

_____

MIRROR QUESTIONS

● Is it true that your organization plans to lay off 20 percent of its workforce by the end of the year?

_____

_____

_____

_____

● I understand your CEO is likely to be indicted by the grand jury?

_____

_____

_____

_____

_____

● Has your company been dumping highly toxic waste directly into the groundwater?

_____

_____

_____

_____

_____

Brainstorming More Tough Questions

Now that you've had a taste of the kinds of tough questions you might encounter, and you've practiced using your Transitional Phrases to successfully bridge to your messages, put yourself in the interviewer's shoes for a moment. Brainstorm some questions you might ask your organization's CEO, executive director, or managing partner about real issues facing your organization, and consider how you would respond to these questions.

It's not only a good way to prepare for troublesome questions, but this exercise will also help sharpen your interviewing skills. Now that you know the Tricky Question Types, think how effective you will be when interviewing someone who has not read _Tough Questions—Good Answers_.

Write down the toughest questions you can think of to ask the top executive in your organization. When you're done, answer them yourself.

_____

_____

_____

_____

_____

_____

_____

Personal Messages

In today's highly volatile business climate, you never really know when you might need to look for a new job or when someone might approach you with that "perfect" job opportunity. You also may just be joining the workforce after graduating from college (as my twins did recently). Even though I have you focusing primarily on business-related messages in these exercises, I don't want to leave you with the impression that personal messages are not important. After all, who is more important than YOU?

If you have been completing these exercises with your personal messages in mind, you're ahead of the game. Frankly, I think creating personal messages are harder than developing professional ones because they require you to be highly objective about

yourself, something many of us are not used to doing. However, I have total faith in you.

In this exercise, I want you to apply the same
newfound skills you demonstrated in creating messages about your organization to developing messages
about yourself. Only this time, when you think about
your What, How, and Why messages, consider how
others might see you. Are you a "senior corporate executive with more than twenty years experience"; a
"highly trained computer forensic criminologist with
litigation support experience and a 'Top Secret' clear-
ance"; or "a recent honors graduate in sociology from
a highly respected college or university?"

- **What Message:**

(Example: I am a certified Web designer and
consultant with more than twenty-five years marketing experience in large- and small-corporate and
not-for-profit environments.)

_____

_____

_____

_____

_____

- **How Message:** (Provide some specifics.)

(Example: As a former business manager at one
of the earliest successful social networking commu-
nities and a marketing director for a Fortune 500

company, I am able to advise small businesses in many industries on Web branding, messaging, and design, and help them execute their vision.)

_____

_____

_____

_____

_____

- **Why Message:**

(Example: Because of the depth of my marketing background, I am able to provide small-business clients with large-business expertise in a budget-conscious environment that allows them to grow their Web presence systematically according to their business needs.)

_____

_____

_____

_____

Performance Skills 101

All right. We're rounding the clubhouse turn and heading toward the homestretch. You now know how to create your professional and personal messages and how to use them to take control of any interview. Pretty easy, isn't it? I told you so. From here on out, we're going to look at ways to make you a better performer. By that I mean, we're going to work on techniques that should give you more authority when answering questions, even, God help you, if it's on television.

Watch and Learn

Speaking of television—besides providing news, sports, and entertainment programming— TV can help you become better at answering questions. As I have mentioned elsewhere in *Tough Questions— Good Answers*, you can learn a lot watching newsmakers answer questions well or poorly on TV talk shows. This is especially true of network morning shows where the experience of the guests varies. Some are extremely good at presenting their messages and responding to tough questions. Others? Let's just say they are less so. As you watch TV (or listen to radio), pay attention to how the "pros" answer tough questions. Make a mental note or write down examples of really good or really bad answers to interviewers' questions. See if you can tell what makes one answer better than another.

_____

_____

_____

_____

_____

_____

_____

_____

_____

Dress for Success

As long as you're making a point of watching TV, also pay attention to what people are wearing and what different "looks" communicate. What did I tell you about dangly jewelry and plaid jackets? Even though it's not the topic of this book, much has been written about nonverbal communication. What you wear says a lot about you. Keep a list of "looks" you think work on TV and "looks" that do not. Even if you never do an interview on television, you may be surprised by how much you learn about your own personal style by watching the styles of others.

_____

_____

_____

_____

_____

_____

_____

_____

_____

Say It Like You Mean It

Some are blessed with a voice like John Houseman, Sean Connery, or Patrick Stewart. Most of us mortals are not. But surprisingly, you can put a lot of power behind your voice by simply standing when you speak. For the next week, try standing when you're on an important call. Better yet, use a wireless headset if you can. This will give you freedom to move around and make you more comfortable as you speak. Note the differences. After that, you probably won't be surprised to find yourself standing as often as possible when you need to speak with power and conviction.

Write It Like You Say It

More and more of us are writing for blogs, wikis, or websites. Even though these forums have a more casual or impromptu feel, you still need to communicate what you want to say through clear messages. In the first part of this exercise, write the copy for the homepage of your company's website. (Don't look at what is already there.) Remember, visitors are always asking themselves tough questions about these sites: What is this? Why should I care? Is the information on this site credible?

_____

_____

_____

_____

_____

_____

_____

_____

_____

_____

_____

_____

_____

Now, if you were to create your own blog, what would the homepage look like? What messages would you want to launch into cyberspace? If you're not ready to really put yourself "out there" yet, write about your hobbies or some other benign interest. Again, remember, you need to communicate what you want to say in a way that will make visitors stick around. It can be breezy, funny, provocative, or challenging, but it needs to say something. The best way to ensure that your website or blog contribution meets its goal is to know what message(s) you want to communicate.

_____

_____

_____

_____

_____

_____

I hope these exercises were helpful to you. Think about your messages and practice using them. Also, begin creating messages for other areas of your professional and personal life. What are the messages for your upcoming product launch? What messages will you use during next year's college admissions interviews? What messages will persuade him or her to go out with you?

The secret to answering any questions successfully and to taking control of any interview is in your hands. (I suddenly feel like I'm talking to Harry Potter.) With practice, the techniques in this book will become second nature to you, and in time, you may even prove to be an oratorical wizard of the first degree.

Interview "Quick Guide" to Review Before a Media Interview

Be Prepared

- Make sure your public relations staff knows about the interview.
- If you unexpectedly receive a call from a reporter, tell them you'll call them back shortly.
- Give yourself at least ten to fifteen minutes before ANY interview to think about your messages, especially if you're working on an unrelated subject immediately beforehand.
- Review your messages or prepare new ones depending upon the subject of the interview.
- Messages: What, How, and Why

Bridge to Your Messages

Use messages to:

- Respond to Open-Ended questions
- Reinforce key thoughts
- Answer tricky questions

Watch Out for Tricky Question Types

Tricky questions include:

- Open-Ended questions
- Loaded-Preface questions
- What-If (Speculative) questions
- A-or-B questions
- Third-Party questions
- Mirror questions

Be Cautious

- A reporter is not your friend.
- You are ALWAYS on the record.
- Stick to your messages; an interview is not a time for original thought.
- Be respectful and friendly, but you have rights too.
- Beware of a "post-interview high."

Use Words People Can Understand

- Don't use technical jargon or industry nomenclature.
- Use examples to illustrate a point and "word pictures" to make your examples clear.
- Think of the words you would use to explain the subject to an elderly friend or relative.

Look Good and Sound Good

Television interviews:

- Do not wear intricate or loud-print clothing.

- Avoid white shirts or blouses.
- Do not wear large, distracting jewelry.
- Sit comfortably in your chair and lean forward slightly at the waist to show your interest in the interview.
- Feel free to gesture as you would in normal conversation.
- Look at the interviewer, not the camera.
- Keep your answers relatively short, but make sure to work in your messages.
- Assume you are ALWAYS on camera and that your microphone is ALWAYS turned on.

Radio interviews:

- If you're doing a telephone interview, which most radio interviews are, stand up during the interview to release nervous energy and to enhance the sound of your voice.
- Use notes only if you're confident you won't use them as a crutch.
- Do not attempt to memorize what you're going to say.
- Be sure to smile because listeners can "hear" a smile over the radio.

ABOUT THE AUTHOR

Tom Calcagni is a senior communications counselor with more than twenty years of experience in public relations, public affairs, and broadcast journalism. He currently serves as chief communications strategist for the Special Libraries Association (SLA) in Alexandria, Virginia.

Prior to assuming his position at SLA, Calcagni was the senior-most pubic relations executive at the national office of the American Automobile Association. During his tenure at AAA, the association won a coveted Silver Anvil Award from the Public Relations Society of America, one of only a handful of companies to win a Silver Anvil without the involvement of a major public relations firm.

Before joining AAA, Calcagni was senior vice president of B2B technology at MWW/Seattle, a strategic communications firm. He also served as director of corporate communications at CyberCash, Inc., a pioneering Internet payments company headquartered in Reston, Virginia, and was a vice president at Ruder-Finn, Washington, where he helped lead the Institutional Practice Group at the Washington, DC-based public relations firm.

His Washington experience also includes positions as director of communications for former U.S. Senator Robert Stafford of Vermont, chairman of the Senate Environment and Public Works Committee, and for Senator Kay Bailey Hutchison of Texas.

Calcagni is an award-winning television journalist who worked as a reporter and anchor at network-affiliated television stations in Virginia, North Carolina, Massachusetts, and New York. His reporting was televised frequently on CNN.

He opened Calcagni Media Coaching (www.calcagnimediacoaching.com) in 2001 and continues to provide media coaching to corporate and not-for-profit executives throughout the United States.

Calcagni received his BA in history at Middlebury College and earned an MSJ at the Medill School of Journalism at Northwestern University.

He and his wife, Elizabeth, live in Northern Virginia.